Margaret of Anjou

Margaret of Anjou

Makers of History Series

Jacob Abbott

Cedar Lake Classics

Copyright © 2023 by Cedar Lake Classics

This is an annotated edition of a public domain work.

CONTENTS

PHOTO INSERT	vii
PHOTO INSERT	viii
PREFACE	ix

1	The Houses of York and Lancaster	1
2	Manners and Customs of the Time	9
3	King Henry VI	19
4	Margaret's Father and Mother	26
5	Royal Courtship	35
6	The Wedding	46
7	Reception in England	58
8	The Story of Lady Neville	64
9	Plottings	75
10	The Fall of Gloucester	83
11	The Fall of Suffolk	90
12	Birth of a Prince	99

CONTENTS

13	Illness of the King	105
14	Anxiety and Trouble	110
15	Margaret a Fugitive	118
16	Margaret Triumphant	123
17	Margaret in Exile	127
18	A Royal Cousin	131
19	Return to England	137
20	Years of Exile	146
21	The Reconciliation with Warwick	151
22	Bitter Disappointment	155
23	Childless, and a Widow	160
24	Conclusion	167

ABOUT JACOB ABBOTT 173
BIOGRAPHIES ABBOTT WROTE 175

The Bridal Procession

Map Illustrating the History of Margaret of Anjou

PREFACE

THE story of Margaret of Anjou forms a part of the history of England, for the lady, though of Continental origin, was the queen of one of the English kings, and England was the scene of her most remarkable adventures and exploits. She lived in very stormy times, and led a very stormy life; and her history, besides the interest which it excites from the extraordinary personal and political vicissitudes which it records, is also useful in throwing a great deal of light upon the ideas of right and wrong, and of good and evil, and upon the manners and customs, both of peace and war, which prevailed in England during the age of chivalry.

1

The Houses of York and Lancaster

MARGARET OF ANJOU was a heroine; not a heroine of romance and fiction, but of stern and terrible reality. Her life was a series of military exploits, attended with dangers, privations, sufferings, and wonderful vicissitudes of fortune, scarcely to be paralleled in the whole history of mankind.

She was born and lived in a period during which there prevailed in the western part of Europe two great and dreadful quarrels, which lasted for more than a hundred years, and which kept France and England, and all the countries contiguous to them, in a state of continual commotion during all that time.

The first of these quarrels grew out of a dispute which arose among the various branches of the royal family of England in respect to the succession to the crown. The two principal branches of the family were the descendants respectively of the Dukes of York and Lancaster, and the wars which they waged against each other are called in history the wars of the houses of York and Lancaster. These wars continued for several successive generations, and Margaret of Anjou was the queen of one of the most prominent representatives of the Lancaster line. Thus she became most intimately involved in the quarrel.

The second great contention which prevailed during this period consisted of the wars waged between France and England for the possession of the territory which now forms the northern portion of France. A large portion of that territory, during the reigns that immediately preceded the time of Margaret of Anjou, had belonged to England. But the kings of France were continually attempting to regain possession of it—the English, of course, all the time making desperate resistance. Thus, for a hundred years, including the time while Margaret lived, England was involved in a double set of wars—the one internal, being waged by one branch of the royal family against the other for the possession of the throne, and the other external, being waged against France and other Continental powers for the possession of the towns and castles, and the country dependent upon them, which lay along the southern shore of the English Channel.

In order that the story of Margaret of Anjou may be properly understood, it will be necessary first to give some explanations in respect to the nature of these two quarrels, and to the progress which had been made in them up to the time when Margaret came upon the stage. We shall begin with the internal or civil wars which were waged between the families of York and Lancaster. Some account of the origin and nature of this difficulty is given in our history of Richard III., but it is necessary to allude to it again here, and to state some additional particulars in respect to it, on account of the very important part which Margaret of Anjou performed in the quarrel.

The difficulty originated among the children and descendants of King Edward III. He reigned in the early part of the fourteenth century. He occupied the throne a long time, and his reign was considered very prosperous and glorious. The prosperity and glory of it consisted, in a great measure, in the success of the wars which he waged in France, and in the towns, and castles, and districts of country which he conquered there, and annexed to the English domain.

In these wars old King Edward was assisted very much by the princes his sons, who were very warlike young men, and who were engaged from time to time in many victorious campaigns on the Continent. They began this career when they were very young, and they continued it through all the years of their manhood and middle life, for their father lived to an advanced age.

The most remarkable of these warlike princes were Edward and John. Edward was the oldest son, and John the third in order of age of those who arrived at maturity. The name of the second was Lionel. Edward, the oldest son, was of course the Prince of Wales; but, to distinguish him from other Princes of Wales that preceded and followed him, he is known commonly in history by the name of the Black Prince. He received this name originally on account of something about his armor which was black, and which marked his appearance among the other knights on the field of battle.

The Black Prince did not live to succeed his father and inherit the throne, for he lost his health in his campaigns on the Continent, and came home to England, and died a few years before his father died. His son, whose name was Richard, was his heir, and when at length old King Edward died, this young Richard succeeded to the crown, under the title of King Richard II. In the history of Richard II., in this series, a full account of the life of his father, the Black Prince, is given, and of the various remarkable adventures that he met with in his Continental campaigns.

Prince John, the third of the sons of old King Edward, is commonly known in history as John of Gaunt. This word Gaunt was the nearest approach that the English people could make in those days to the pronunciation of the word Ghent, the name of the town where John was born. For King Edward, in the early part of his life, was accustomed to take all his family with him in his Continental campaigns, and so his several children were born in different places, one in one city and another in another, and many of them received names from the places where they happened to be born.

On the following page we have a genealogical table of the family of Edward III. At the head of it we have the names of Edward III. and Philippa his wife. In a line below are the names of those four of his sons whose descendants figure in English history. It was among the descendants of these sons that the celebrated wars between the houses of York and Lancaster, called the wars of the roses, arose.

These wars were called the wars of the roses from the circumstance that the white and the red rose happened in some way to be chosen as the badges of the two parties

Selecting the Roses

—the white rose being that of the house of York, and the red that of the house of Lancaster.

The reader will observe that the dukes of Lancaster and York are the third and fourth of the brothers enumerated in the table, where, as it might have been supposed that any contest which should have arisen in respect to the crown would have taken place between families of the first and second. But the first and second sons and their descendants were soon set aside, as it were, from the competition, in the following manner.

The line of the first brother soon became extinct. Edward himself, the Prince of Wales, died during his father's lifetime, leaving his son Richard as his heir. Then, when the old king died, Richard succeeded him. As he was the oldest living son of the oldest son, his claim could not be disputed, and so his uncles acquiesced in it. They wished very much, it is true, to govern the realm, but they contented themselves with ruling in Richard's name until he became of age, and then Richard took the government into his own hands. The country was tolerably well satisfied under his dominion for some years, but at length Richard became dissipated and vicious, and he domineered over the people of England in so haughty a manner, and oppressed them so severely by the taxes and other exactions which he laid upon them, that a very general discontent prevailed at last against him and against his government. This discontent would have given either of his uncles a great advantage in any design which they might have formed to take away the crown from him. As it was, it greatly increased their power and influence in the land, and diminished, in a corresponding degree, that of the king. The uncles appear to have been contented with this share of power and influence, which seemed naturally to fall into their hands, and did not attempt any open rebellion.

Richard had a cousin, however, a young man of just about his own age, who was driven at last, by a peculiar train of circumstances, to rise against him. This cousin was the son of his uncle John. His name was Henry Bolingbroke. He appears in the genealogical table as Henry IV., that having been his title subsequently as King of England.

This cousin Henry became involved in a quarrel with a certain nobleman named Norfolk. Indeed, the nobles of those days were continually getting engaged in feuds and quarrels, which they fought out with the greatest recklessness, sometimes by regular battles between armies of retainers, and sometimes by single combat, in which the parties to the dispute were supposed to appeal to Almighty God, who they believed, or professed to believe, would give the victory to the just side in the quarrel. These single combats were arranged with great ceremony and parade, and were performed in a very public and solemn manner; being, in fact, a recognized and established part of the system of public law as administered in those days. In the next chapter, when speaking more particularly of the manners and customs of the times, I shall give an account in full of one of these duels. I have only to say here that Richard, on hearing of the quarrel between his cousin Henry and Norfolk, decreed that they should settle it by single combat, and preparations were accordingly made for the trial, and the parties appeared, armed and equipped for the fight, in the presence of an immense concourse of people assembled to witness the spectacle. The king himself was to preside on the occasion.

But just before the signal was to be given for the combat to begin, the king interrupted the proceedings, and declared that he would decide the question himself. He pronounced both the combatants guilty, and issued a decree of banishment against both. Henry submitted, and both prepared to leave the country. These transactions, of course, attracted great attention throughout England, and they operated to bring Henry forward in a very conspicuous manner before the people of the realm. He was in the direct line of succession to the crown, and he was, moreover, a prince of great wealth, and of immense personal influence, and so, just in proportion as Richard himself was disliked, Henry would naturally become an object of popular sympathy and regard. When he set out on his journey toward the southern coast, in order to leave the country in pursuance of his sentence, the people flocked along the waysides, and assembled in the towns where he passed, as if he were a conqueror returning from his victories instead of a condemned criminal going into banishment.

Soon after this, the Duke of Lancaster, Henry's father, died, and then Richard, instead of allowing his cousin to succeed to the immense estates which his father left, confiscated all the property, under the pretext that Henry had forfeited it, and so converted it to his own use. This last outrage aroused Henry to such a pitch of indignation that he resolved to invade England, depose Richard, and claim the crown for himself.

This plan was carried into effect. Henry raised an armament, crossed the Channel, and landed in England. The people took sides. A great majority sided with Henry. A full account of this insurrection and invasion is given in our history of Richard II. All that it is necessary to say here is that the revolution was effected. Richard was deposed, and

Henry obtained possession of the kingdom. It was thus that the house of Lancaster first became established on the throne.

But you will very naturally wonder where the representatives of the second brother in Edward the Third's family were all this time, and why, when Richard was deposed, who was the son of the first brother, they did not appear, and advance their claims in competition with Henry. The reason was because there was no male heir of that branch living in that line. You will see by referring again to the table that the only child of Lionel, the second brother, was Philippa, a girl. She had a son, it is true, Roger Mortimer, as appears by the table; but he was yet very young, and could do nothing to assert the claims of his line. Besides, Henry pretended that, together with his claims to the throne through his father, he had others more ancient and better founded still through his mother, who, as he attempted to prove, was descended from an English king who reigned before Edward III. The people of England, as they wished to have Henry for king, were very easily satisfied with his arguments, and so it was settled that he should reign. The line of this second brother, however, did not give up their claims, but reserved them, intending to rise and assert them on the very first favorable opportunity.

Henry reigned about thirteen years, and then was succeeded by his son, Henry V., as appears by the table. There was no attempt to disturb the Lancastrian line in their possession of the throne during these two reigns. The attention, both of the kings and of the people, during all this period, was almost wholly engrossed in the wars which they were waging in France. These wars were very successful. The English conquered province after province and castle after castle, until at length almost the whole country was brought under their sway.

This state of things continued until the death of Henry V., which took place in 1422. He left for his heir a little son, named also Henry, then only about nine months old. This infant was at once invested with the royal authority as King of England and France, under the title of Henry VI., as seen by the table. It was this Henry who, when he arrived at maturity, became the husband of Margaret of Anjou, the subject of this volume. It was during his reign, too, that the first effective attempt was made to dispute the right of the house of Lancaster to the throne, and it was in the terrible contests which this attempt brought on that Margaret displayed the extraordinary military heroism for which she became so renowned. I shall relate the early history of this king, and explain the nature of the combination which was formed during his reign against the Lancastrian line, in a subsequent chapter, after first giving a brief account of such of the manners and customs of those times as are necessary to a proper understanding of the story.

2

Manners and Customs of the Time

IN the days when Margaret of Anjou lived, the kings, princes, nobles, and knights who flourished in the realms of England and France, though they were, relatively to the mass of the people, far more wealthy, proud, and powerful than their successors are at the present day, still lived in many respects in a very rude and barbarous manner. They enjoyed very few of the benefits and privileges which all classes enjoy in the age in which we live. They had very few books, and very little advantage of instruction to enable them to read those that they had. There were no good roads by which they could travel comfortably from place to place, and no wheeled carriages. They lived in castles, very strongly built indeed, and very grand and picturesque sometimes in external appearance, but very illy furnished and comfortless within. The artisans were skillful in fabricating splendid caparisons for the horses, and costly suits of glittering armor for the men, and the architects could construct grand cathedrals, and ornament them with sculptures and columns which are the wonder of the present age. But in respect to all the ordinary means and appliances of daily life, even the most wealthy and powerful nobles lived in a very barbarous way.

The mass of the common people were held in a state of abject submission to the will of the chieftains, very much in the condition of slaves, being compelled to toil in the cultivation of their masters' lands, or to go out as soldiers to fight in their quarrels, without receiving any compensation. The great ambition of every noble and knight was to have as many of these retainers as possible under his command. The only limit to the number which each chieftain could assemble was his power of feeding them. For in those days men could be more easily found to fight than to engage in any other employment, and there were great numbers always ready to follow any commander who was able to maintain them.

Each great noble lived in state in his castle, like a prince or a petty king. Those of the highest class had their privy councilors, treasurers, marshals, constables, stewards, secretaries, heralds, pursuivants, pages, guards, trumpeters—in short, all the various officers that were to be found in the court of the sovereign. To these were added whole bands of minstrels, mimics, jugglers, tumblers, rope-dancers, and buffoons. Besides these, there was always attached to great each castle a large company of priests and monks, who performed divine service according to the usages of those times, in a gorgeously-decorated chapel built for this purpose within the castle walls.

Thus the whole country was divided, as it were, into a vast number of separate jurisdictions, each with an earl, or a baron, or a duke at the head of it, who ruled with an almost absolute sway in every thing that related to the internal management of his province, while however, he recognized a certain general dominion over all on the part of the king. Such being the state of the case, it is not surprising that the nobles were often powerful enough, as will course of this narrative, to band together and set up and put down kings at their pleasure.

Perhaps the most powerful of all the great nobles who flourished during the time of Margaret of Anjou was the Earl of Warwick. So great was his influence in deciding between the rival claims of different pretenders to the crown, that he is known in history by the title of the King-maker. His wealth was so enormous that it was said that the body of retainers that he maintained amounted sometimes in number to thirty thousand men.

The employments, and even the amusements of these great barons and nobles, were all military. They looked down with great disdain upon all the useful pursuits of art and industry, regarding them as only fit occupations for serfs and slaves. Their business was going to war, either independently against each other, or, under the command of the king, against some common enemy. When they were not engaged in any of these wars they amused themselves and the people of their courts with tournaments, and mock combats and encounters of all kinds, which they arranged in open grounds contiguous to their castles with great pomp and parade.

It could not be expected that such powerful and warlike chieftains as these could be kept much under the control of law by the ordinary machinery of courts of justice. There were, of course, laws and courts of justice in those days, but they were administered chiefly upon the common people, for the repression of common crimes. The nobles, in their quarrels and contentions with each other, were accustomed to settle the questions that arose in other ways. Sometimes they did this by marshaling their troops and fighting each other in regular campaigns, during which they laid siege to castles, and ravaged villages and fields, as in times of public war. Sometimes, when the power of the king was sufficient to prevent such out-breaks as these, the parties to the quarrel were summoned to settle the dispute by single combat in the presence of the king and his court, as well as of a vast multitude of assembled spectators. These single combats were the origin of the modern custom of dueling.

At the present day, the settlement of disputes by a private combat between the parties to it is made a crime by the laws of the land. It is justly considered a barbarous and sense-less practice. The man who provokes another to a duel and then kills him in the fight, instead of acquiring any glory by the deed, has to bear, for the rest of his life, both in his own conscience and in the opinion of mankind, the mark and stain of murder. And when, in defiance of law, and of the opinions and wishes of all good men, any two disputants who have become involved in a quarrel are rendered so desperate by their angry passions as to desire to satisfy them by this mode, they are obliged to resort to all sorts of manoeuvres and stratagems to conceal the crime which they are about to commit, and to avoid the interference of their friends or of the officers of the law.

Ordeal Combat

In the days, however, of the semi-savage knights and barons who flourished so luxuriantly in the times of which we are writing, the settlement of a dispute by single combat between the two parties to it was an openly recognized and perfectly legitimate mode of arbitration, and the trial of the question was conducted with forms and ceremonies even more strict and more solemn than those which governed the proceedings in regular courts of justice.

The engraving on the preceding page is a sort of rude emblematic representation of such a trial, copied from a drawing in an ancient manuscript. We see the combatants in the foreground, with the judges and spectators behind.

It was to a public and solemn combat of this kind that Richard the Second summoned his cousin Henry Bolingbroke, and his enemy, as related in the last chapter. In that instance the combat was not fought, the king having taken the case into his own hands, and condemned both the parties before the contest was begun. But in multitudes of other cases the trial was carried through to its consummation in the death of one party, and the triumph and acquittal of the other.

Very many detailed and full accounts of these combats have come down to us in the writings of the ancient chroniclers. I will here give a description of one of them, as an example of this mode of trial, which was fought in the public square in front of King Richard the Second's palace, the king himself, all the principal nobles of the court, and a great crowd of other persons being provided with seats around the area as spectators of the fight. The nobles and knights were all dressed in complete armor; and heralds, and squires, and guards were stationed in great numbers to regulate the proceedings. It was on a bright morning in June when the combat was fought, and the whole aspect of the scene was that of a grand and joyful spectacle on a gala day.

It was estimated that more people from the surrounding country came to London on the occasion of this duel than at the time of the coronation of the king. It took place about three years after the coronation.

The parties to the combat were John Anneslie, a knight, and Thomas Katrington, a squire. Anneslie, the knight, was the complainant and the challenger. Katrington, the squire, was the defendant. The circumstances of the case were as follows.

Katrington, the squire, was governor of a castle in Normandy. The castle belonged to a certain English knight who afterward died, and his estate descended to Anneslie, the complainant in this quarrel. If the squire had successfully defended the castle from the French who attacked it, then it would have descended with the other property to Anneslie. But he did not. When the French came and laid siege to the castle, Katrington surrendered it, and so it was lost. He maintained that he had not a sufficient force to defend it, and that he had no alternative but to surrender. Anneslie, on the other hand, alleged that he might have defended it, and that be would have done so if he had been faithful to his trust; but that he had been bribed by the French to give it up. This Katrington denied; so Anneslie, who was very angry at the loss of the castle, challenged him to single combat to try the question.

It is plain that this was a very absurd way of attempting to ascertain whether Katrington had or had not been bribed; but, as the affair had occurred some years before, and in another country, and as, moreover, the giving and receiving of bribes are facts always very difficult to be proved by ordinary evidence, it was decided by the government of the king that this was a proper case for the trial by combat, and both parties were ordered to prepare for the fight. The day, too, was fixed, and the place—the public square opposite the king's palace—was appointed. As the time drew nigh, the whole country for many miles around was excited to the highest pitch of interest and expectation.

At the place where the combat was to be fought a large space was railed in by a very substantial barricade. The barricade was made very strong, so as to resist the utmost possible pressure of the crowd. Elevated seats, commanding a full view of the lists, as the area railed in was called, were erected for the use of the king and the nobles of the court, and all other necessary preparations were made. When the hour arrived on the appointed day, the king and the nobles came in great state and took their places. The whole square, with the exception of the lists and proper avenues of approach, which were kept open by the men-at-arms, had long since, been filled with an immense crowd of people from the surrounding country. At length, after a brief period of expectation, the challenger, Anneslie, was seen coming along one of the approaches, mounted on a horse splendidly caparisoned, and attended by several knights and squires, his friends, all completely armed.

He stopped when he reached the railing and dismounted from his horse. It was against the laws of the combat for either party to enter the lists mounted. If a horse went within the inclosure he was forfeited by that act to a certain public officer called the high constable of England, who was responsible for the regularity and order of the proceedings.

Anneslie, having thus dismounted from his horse with the assistance of his attendants, walked into the lists all armed and equipped for the fight. His squires attended him. He walked there to and fro a few minutes, and then a herald, blowing a trumpet, summoned the accused to appear.

"Thomas Katrington! Thomas Katrington!" he cried out in a loud voice, "come and appear, to save the action for which Sir John Anneslie, knight, hath publicly and by writing appealed thee!"

Three times the herald proclaimed this summons, At the third time Katrington appeared.

He came, as Anneslie had come, mounted upon a war-horse splendidly caparisoned, and with his arms embroidered on the trappings. He was attended by his friends, the representatives of the seconds of the modern duel. The two stopped at the entrance of the lists, and dismounting, passed into the lists on foot. Every body being now intent on the combatants, the horse for the moment was let go, and, being eager to follow his master, he ran up and down along the railing, reaching his head and neck over as far as he could, and trying to get over. At length he was taken and led away; but the lord high constable said at once that he should claim him for having entered the lists.

"At least," said he, "I shall claim his head and neck, and as much of him as was over the railing."

The combatants now stood confronting each other within the lists. A written document was produced, which had been prepared, as was said, by consent of both parties, containing a statement of the charge made against Katrington, namely, that of treason, in having betrayed to the enemy for money a castle intrusted to his charge, and his reply. The herald read this document with a loud voice, in order that all the assembly, or as many as possible, might hear it. As soon as it was read, Katrington began to take exceptions to some passages in it. The Duke of Lancaster, who seemed to preside on the occasion, put an end to his criticisms at once, saying that he had already agreed to the paper, and that now, if he made any difficulty about it, and refused to fight, he should be adjudged guilty of the treason, and should at once be led out to execution.

Katrington then said that he was ready to fight his antagonist, not only on the points raised in the document which had been read, but on any and all other points whatever that might be laid to his charge. He had entire confidence, he said, that the justice of his cause would secure him the victory.

The next proceeding in this strange ceremony was singular enough. It was the solemn administering of an oath to each of the combatants, by which oath they severally swore that the cause in which they were to fight was true, and that they did not deal in any witchcraft or magic art, by which they expected to gain the victory over their adversary; and also, that they had not about their persons any herb or stone, or charm of any kind, by which they hoped to obtain any advantage.

After this oath had been administered, time was allowed for the combatants to say their prayers. This ceremony they performed apparently in a very devout manner, and then the battle began.

The combatants fought first with spears, then with swords, and finally, coming to very close quarters, with daggers. Anneslie seemed to gain the advantage. He succeeded in disarming Katrington of one after another of his weapons, and finally threw him down. When Katrington was down, Anneslie attempted to throw himself upon him, in order to crush him with the weight of his heavy iron armor. But he was exhausted by the heat and by the exertion which he had made, and the perspiration running down from his forehead under his helmet blinded his eyes, so that he could not see exactly where Katrington was, and, instead of falling upon him, he came down upon the ground at a little distance away. Katrington then contrived to make his way to Anneslie and to get upon him, thus pressing him down to the ground with his weight. The combatants lay thus a few minutes locked together on the ground, and struggling with each other as well as their heavy and cumbrous armor would permit, Katrington being all the time uppermost, when the king at length gave orders that the contest should cease and that the men should be separated.

In obedience to these orders, some men came to rescue Anneslie by taking Katrington off from him. But Anneslie begged them not to interfere. And when the men had taken Katrington off, he urged them to place him back upon him again as he was before, for he said he himself was not hurt at all, and he had no doubt that he should gain the victory if they would leave him alone. The men, however, having the king's order for what they were doing, paid no heed to Anneslie's requests, but proceeded to lead Katrington away.

They found that he was so weak and exhausted that he could not stand. They led him to a chair, and then; taking off his helmet, they tried to revive him by bathing his face and giving him some wine.

In the mean time, Anneslie, finding that Katrington was taken away, allowed himself to be lifted up. When set upon his feet, he walked along toward the part of the inclosure which was near the king's seat, and begged the king to allow the combat to proceed. He said he was sure that he should obtain the victory if they would but permit him to continue the combat to the end. Finally the king and nobles gave their consent, and ordered that Anneslie should be placed upon the ground again, and Katrington upon him, in the same position, as nearly as possible, as before.

But on going again to Katrington with a view of executing this decree, they found that he was in such a condition as to preclude the possibility of it. He had fainted and fallen down out of his chair in a deadly swoon. He seemed not to be wounded, but to be utterly exhausted by the heat, the weight of his armor, and the extreme violence of the exertion which he had made. His friends raised him up again, and proceeded to unbuckle and take off his armor. Relieved from this burden, he began to come to himself. He opened his eyes and looked around, staring with a wild, bewildered, and ghastly look, which moved the pity of all the beholders, that is, of all but Anneslie. He, on leaving the king, came to where poor Katrington was sitting, and, full of rage and hate, began to taunt and revile him, calling him traitor, and false, perjured villain, and daring him to come out again into the area and finish the fight.

To this Katrington made no answer, but stared wildly about with a crazed look, as if he did not know where he was or what they were doing to him.

So the farther prosecution of the combat was relinquished. Anneslie was declared the victor, and poor Katrington was deemed to be proved, by his defeat, guilty of the treason which had been charged against him. He was borne away by his friends, and put into his bed. He continued delirious all that night, and the next morning at nine o'clock he died.

Thus was this combat fought, as the ancient historian says, to the great rejoicing of the common people and the discouragement of traitors!

3

King Henry VI

KING HENRY THE SIXTH, who subsequently became the husband of Margaret of Anjou, was only about nine months old, as has already been said, when he succeeded to the throne by the death of his father. He was proclaimed by the heralds to the sound of trumpets and drums, in all parts of London, while he was yet an infant in his nurse's arms.

Of course the question was now who should have the rule in England while Henry remained a child. And this question chiefly affected the little king's uncles, of whom there were three—all rude, turbulent, and powerful nobles, such as were briefly described in the last chapter. Each of them had a powerful band of retainers and partisans attached to his service, and the whole kingdom dreaded greatly the quarrels which every one knew were now likely to break out.

The oldest of these uncles was Thomas. He was Duke of Exeter.

The second was John. He was Duke of Bedford. The third was Humphrey. He was Duke of Gloucester. Thomas and Humphrey seem to have been in England at the time of their brother the old king's death. John, or Bedford, as he was commonly called, was in France, where he had been pursuing a very renowned and successful career, in extending and maintaining the English conquests in that country.

The leading nobles and officers of the government were assembled in council soon after the old king's death, and in order to prevent the breaking out of the quarrels which were otherwise to have been anticipated between these uncles, they determined to divide the power as nearly as possible in an equal manner among them. So they appointed Thomas, the Duke of Exeter, who seems to have been less ambitious and warlike in his character than the rest, to the charge and custody of the young king's person. Humphrey, the Duke of Gloucester, was made Protector of England, and John, the Duke of Bedford, the Regent of France. Thus they were all seemingly satisfied.

But the peace which resulted from this arrangement did not continue very long. Pretty soon a certain Henry Beaufort, a bishop, was appointed to be associated with Henry's uncle Thomas in the personal charge of the king. This Henry Beaufort was Henry's great-uncle, being one of the sons of John of Gaunt. He was a younger son of his father, and so was brought up to the Church, and had been appointed Bishop of Winchester, and afterward made a cardinal. Thus he occupied a very exalted position, and possessed a degree of wealth, and power, and general consequence little inferior to those of the grandest nobles in the land. He was a man, too, of great capacity, very skillful in manoeuvring and intriguing, and he immediately began to form ambitious schemes for himself which he designed to carry into effect through the power which the custody of the young king gave him. He was, of course, very jealous of the influence and power of the Duke of Gloucester, and the Duke of Gloucester became very jealous of him. It was not long before occasions arose which brought the two men, and their bands of followers, into direct and open collision.

I can not here go into a full account of the particulars of the quarrel. One of the first difficulties was about the Tower of London, which Beaufort had under his command, and where there was a prisoner whom Gloucester wished to set at liberty. Then there was a great riot and disturbance on London Bridge, which threw the whole city of London into a state of alarm. Beaufort alleged that Gloucester had formed a plan to seize the person of the king and tale him away from Beaufort's custody; and that he had designs, moreover, on Beaufort's life. To defend himself and, to prevent Gloucester from coming to the palace where he was residing, he seized and fortified the passages leading to the bridge. He built barricades, and took down the chains of the portcullis, and assembled a large armed force to guard the point. The people of London were in great alarm. They set watches day and night to protect their property from the anticipated violence of the soldiers and partisans of the combatants, and thus all was commotion and fear. Of course there were no courts of justice powerful enough to control such a contest as this, and finally the people sent off a delegation to the Duke of Bedford in France, imploring him to come to England immediately and see if he could not settle the quarrel.

The Duke of Bedford came. A Parliament was convened, and the questions at issue between the two great disputants were brought to a solemn trial. The Duke of Gloucester made out a series of heavy charges against the cardinal, and the cardinal made a formal reply which contained not only his defense, but also counter charges against the duke. These papers were drawn up with great technicality and ceremony by the lawyers employed on each side to manage the case, and were submitted to the Duke of Bedford and to the Parliament. A series of debates ensued, in which the friends of the two parties respectively brought criminations and recriminations against each other without end. The result was, as is usual in such cases, that both sides appeared to have been to blame, and in order to settle the dispute a sort of compromise was effected, with which both parties professed to be satisfied, and a reconciliation, or what outwardly appeared to be such, was made. A new division of powers and prerogatives between Gloucester, as Protector of England, and Beaufort, as custodian of the king, was arranged, and peace being thus restored, Bedford went back again to France.

Things went on tolerably well after this for many years; that is, there were no more open outbreaks, though the old jealousy and hatred between Gloucester and the cardinal still continued. The influence of the Duke of Bedford held both parties in check as long as the duke lived. At length, however, when the young king was about fourteen years old, the

Duke of Bedford died. He was in France at the time of his death. He was buried with great pomp and ceremony in the city of Rouen, which had been in some sense the head-quarters of his dominion in that country, and a splendid monument was erected over his tomb:

A curious anecdote is related of the King of France in relation to this tomb. Some time after the tomb was built Rouen fell into the hands of the French, and some persons proposed to break down the monument which had been built in memory of their old enemy; but the King of France would not listen to the proposal.

"What honor shall it be to us," said he, "or to you, to break down the monument, or to pull out of the ground the dead bones of him whom, in his life, neither my father nor your progenitors, with all their power, influence, and friends, were ever able to make flee one foot backward, but who, by his strength, wit, and policy, kept them all at bay. Wherefore I say, let God have his soul; and for his body, let it rest in peace where they have laid it."

When King Henry was old enough to be crowned, in addition to the English part of the ceremony, he went to France to receive the crown of that country too. The ceremony, as is usual with the French kings, was performed at the town of St. Denis, near Paris, where is an ancient royal chapel, in which all the great religious ceremonies connected with the French monarchy have been performed. A very curious account is given by the ancient chroniclers of the pageants and ceremonies which were enacted on this occasion. The king proceeded into France and journeyed to St. Denis at the head of a grand cavalcade of knights, nobles, and men-at-arms, amounting to many thousand men, all of whom were adorned with dresses and trappings of the most gorgeous description. At St. Denis the authorities came out to meet the king, dressed in robes of vermilion, and bearing splendid banners. The king was presented, as he passed through the gates, "with three crimson hearts, in one of which were two doves; in another, several small birds, which were let fly over his head; while the third was filled with violets and flowers, which were thrown over the lords that attended and followed him."

At the same place, too, a company of the principal civic dignitaries of the town appeared, bearing a gorgeous canopy of blue silk, adorned and embroidered in the most beautiful manner with royal emblems. This canopy they held over the king as he advanced into the town.

At one place farther on, where there was a little bridge to be crossed, there was a pageant of three savages fighting about a woman in a mimic forest. The savages continued fighting until the king had passed by. Next came a fountain flowing with wine, with mermaids swimming about in it. The wine in this fountain was free to all who chose to come and drink it.

Then, farther still, the royal party came to a place where an artificial forest had been made, by some means or other, in a large, open square. There was a chase going on in this forest at the time when the king went by. The chase consisted of a living stag hunted by real dogs. The stag came and took refuge at the feet of the king's horse, and his majesty saved the poor animal's life.

Thus the king was conducted to his palace. Several days were spent in preliminary pageants and ceremonies like the above, and then the coronation took place in the church, the king and his party being stationed on a large platform raised for the purpose in the most conspicuous part of the edifice.

After the coronation there was a grand banquet, at which the king, with his lords and great officers of state, sat at a marble table in a magnificent ancient hall. Henry Beaufort, the Bishop of Winchester, was the principal personage in all these ceremonies next to the king. Gloucester was very jealous of him, in respect to the conspicuous part which he took in these proceedings.

Henry was quite young at the time of his coronations. He was a very pretty boy, and his countenance wore a mild and gentle expression.

The quarrel between the Duke of Gloucester and the bishop was kept, in some degree, subdued during this period, partly by the influence of the Duke of Bedford while he lived, and partly by Gloucester's mind being taken up to a considerable extent with other things, especially with his campaigns in France; for he was engaged during the period of the king's minority in many important military expeditions in that country. At length, however, he came back to England, and there, when the king was about twenty years of age, the quarrel between him and the bishop's party broke out anew. The king himself was, however, now old enough to take some part in such a difficulty, and so both sides appealed to him. Gloucester made out a series of twenty-four articles of complaint against the bishop. The bishop, on the other hand, accused the duke of treason, and he specially charged that his wife had attempted to destroy the life of the king by witchcraft. The duchess was condemned on this charge, and it is said that, by way of penance, she was sentenced to walk barefoot through the most public street in London with a lighted taper in her hand. Some other persons, who were accused of being accomplices in this crime, were put to death.

Henry VI. in his Youth

The witchcraft which it was said these persons practiced was that of making a waxen image of the king, and then, after connecting it with him in some mysterious and magical way by certain charms and incantations, melting it away by degrees before a slow fire, by which means the king himself, as was supposed, would be caused to pine and wither away, and at last to die. It was universally believed in those days that this could be done.

The Penance

Of course, such proceedings as these only embittered the quarrel more and more, and Gloucester became more resolute and determined than ever in prosecuting his intrigues for depriving the bishop of influence, and for getting the power into his own hands. The king, though he favored the cardinal, was so quiet and gentle in his disposition, and so little disposed to take an active part in such a quarrel, that the bishop could not induce him to act as decidedly as he wished. So he finally conceived the idea of finding some very intelligent and capable princess as a wife for the king, hoping to increase the power which he exercised in the realm through his influence over her.

The lady that he selected for this purpose was Margaret of Anjou.

4

Margaret's Father and Mother

IN former times, the territory which now constitutes France was divided into a great number of separate provinces, each of which formed almost a distinct state or kingdom. These several provinces were the possessions of lords, dukes, and barons, who ruled over them, respectively, like so many petty kings, with almost absolute sway, though they all acknowledged a general allegiance to the kings of France or of England. The more northern provinces pertained to England. Those in the interior and southern portions of the country were under the dominion of France.

The great families who held these provinces as their possessions ruled over them in a very lordly manner. They regarded not only the territory itself which they held, but the right to govern the inhabitants of it as a species of property, which was subject, like any other estate, to descend from parent to child by hereditary right, to be conveyed to another owner by treaty or surrender, to be assigned to a bride as her marriage portion, or to be disposed of in any other way that the lordly proprietors might prefer. These great families took their names from the provinces over which they ruled.

One of these provinces was Anjou. The father of Margaret, the subject of this history, was a celebrated personage named Regnier or René, commonly called King René. He was a younger son of the family which reigned over Anjou. It is from this circumstance that our heroine derives the name by which she is generally designated—Margaret of Anjou. The reason why her father was called King René will appear in the sequel.

Another of the provinces of France above referred to was Lorraine. Lorraine was a large, and beautiful, and very valuable country, situated toward the eastern part of France. Anjou was considerably to the westward of it.

The name of the Duke of Lorraine at this time was Charles. He had a daughter named Isabella. She was the heiress to all her father's possessions. She was a young lady of great beauty, of high spirit, of a very accomplished education, according to the ideas of those times. When René was about fourteen years old a match was arranged between him and Isabella, who was then only about ten. The marriage was celebrated with great parade, and the youthful pair went to reside at a palace called Pont à Mousson, in a grand castle which was given to Isabella by her father as a bridal gift at the time of her marriage. Here it was expected that they would live until the death of her father, when they were to come into possession of the whole province of Lorraine.

In process of time, while living at this castle, René and Isabella had several children. Margaret was the fifth. She was born in 1429. Her birthday was March 23.

The little infant was put under the charge of a family nurse named Theophanie. Theophanie was a long-tried and very faithful domestic. She was successively the nurse to all of Isabella's children, and the family became so much attached to her that when she died René caused a beautiful monument to be raised to her memory. This monument contained a sculptured image of Theophanie, with two of the children in her arms.

Very soon after her birth Margaret was baptized with great pomp in the Cathedral in the town of Toul. A large number of relatives of high rank witnessed and took part in the ceremony.

When at length Charles, Duke of Lorraine, Isabella's father, died, and the province should have descended to Isabella and René, there suddenly appeared another claimant, who thought, not that he had a better right to the province than Isabella, but that he had more power to seize and hold it than she, even with all the aid that her husband René could afford her. This claimant was Isabella's uncle, the younger brother of Duke Charles who had just died. His name was Antoine de Vaudemonte, or, as it would be expressed in English, Anthony of Vaudemont. This uncle, on the death of Isabella's father, determined to seize the duchy for himself, instead of allowing it to descend to Isabella, the proper heir, who, being but a woman, was looked upon with very little respect. "Lorraine," he said, "was too noble and valuable a fief to descend in the family on the spindle side."

So he collected his adherents and retainers, organized an army, and took the field. Isabella, on the other hand, did all in her power to induce the people of the country to espouse her cause. René took the command of the forces which were raised in her behalf, and went forth to meet Antoine. Isabella herself, taking the children with her, went to the city of Nancy —which was then, as now, the chief city of Lorraine, and was consequently the safest place for her—intending to await there the result of the conflict. Little Margaret was at this time about two years old.

The battle was fought at a place called Bulgneville, and the fortune of war, as it would seem, turned in this case against the right, for René's party were entirely defeated, and he himself was wounded and taken prisoner. He fought like a lion, it is said, as long as he remained unharmed; but at last he received a desperate wound on his brow, and the blood from this wound ran down into his eyes and blinded him, so that he could do no more; and he was immediately seized by the men who had wounded him, and made prisoner. The person who thus wounded and captured him was the squire of a certain knight who had espoused the cause of Antoine, named the Count St. Pol.

In the mean time Isabella had remained at Nancy with the children, in a state of the utmost suspense and anxiety, awaiting the result of a conflict on which depended the fate of every thing that was valuable and dear to her. At length, at the window of the tower where she was watching, with little Margaret in her arms, for the coming of a herald from her husband to announce his victory, her heart sank within her to see, instead of a messenger of joy and triumph, a broken crowd of fugitives, breathless and covered with dust and blood, suddenly bursting into view, and showing too plainly by their aspect of terror and distress that all was lost. Isabella was overwhelmed with consternation at the sight. She clasped little Margaret closely in her arms, exclaiming in tones of indescribable agony, "My husband is killed! my husband is killed!"

Her distress and anguish were somewhat calmed by the fugitives assuring her, when they arrived, that her husband was safe, though he had been wounded and taken prisoner.

Distress of Margaret's Mother

There was a great deal of sympathy felt for Isabella in her distress by all the people of Nancy. She was very young and very beautiful. Her children, and especially Margaret, were very beautiful too, and this greatly increased the compassion which the people were disposed to feel for her. Isabella's mother was strongly inclined to make new efforts to raise an army, in order to meet and fight Antoine again; but Isabella herself, who was now more concerned for the safety of her husband than for the recovery of her dominions, was disposed to pursue a conciliatory course. So she sent word to her uncle that she wished to see him, and entreated him to grant her an interview. Antoine acceded to her request, and at the interview Isabella begged her uncle to make peace with her, and to give her back her husband.

Antoine said that it was out of his power to liberate René, for he had delivered him to the custody of the Duke of Burgundy, who had been his ally in the war, and the duke had conveyed him away to his castle at Dijon, and shut him up there, and that now he would probably not be willing to give him up without the payment of a ransom. He said, however, that he was willing to make a truce with Isabella for six months, to give time to see what arrangement could be made.

This truce was agreed upon, and then, at length, after a long negotiation, terms of peace were concluded. René was to pay a large sum to the Duke of Burgundy for his ransom, and, in the mean time, while he was procuring the money, he was to leave his two sons in the duke's hands as hostages, to be held by the duke as security. In respect to Lorraine, Antoine insisted, as another of the conditions of peace, that Isabella's oldest daughter, Yolante, then about nine years old, should be betrothed to his son Frederick, so as to combine, in the next generation at least, the conflicting claims of the two parties to the possession of the territory; and, in order to secure the fulfillment of this condition, Yolante was to be delivered immediately to the charge and custody of Antoine's wife, the mother of her future husband.

Thus all of Isabella's children were taken away from her except Margaret. And even Margaret, though left for the present with her mother, did not escape being involved in the entanglements of the treaty. Antoine insisted that she, too, should be betrothed to one of his partisans; and, as if to make the case as painful and humiliating to René and Isabella as possible, the person chosen to be her future husband was the very Count St. Pol whose squire had cut down and captured René at the battle of Bulgneville.

These conditions were very hard, but Isabella consented to them, as it was only by so doing that any hope seemed to be opened before her of obtaining the release of her husband. And even this hope, in the end, proved delusive. René found that, notwithstanding all his efforts, he could not obtain the money which the duke required for his ransom. Accordingly, in order to save his boys, whom he had delivered to the duke as hostages, he was obliged to return to Dijon and surrender himself again a prisoner. His parting with his wife and children, before going a second time into a confinement to which they could now see no end, was heartrending. Even little Margaret, who was yet so very young, joined from sympathy in the general sorrow, and wept bitterly when her father went away.

The duke confined his captive in an upper room in a high tower of the castle of Dijon, and kept him imprisoned there for several years. One of the boys was kept with him, but the other was set at liberty. All this time Margaret remained with her mother. She was a very beautiful and a very intelligent child, and was a great favorite with all who knew her. The interest which was awakened by her beauty and her other personal attractions was greatly increased by the general sympathy which was felt for the misfortunes of her father, and the loneliness and distress of her mother.

In the mean time, René, shut up in the tower at the castle of Dijon, made himself as contented as he could, and employed his time in various peaceful and ingenious occupations. Though he had fought well in the battle with Antoine, he was, in fact, not at all of a warlike disposition. He was very fond of music, and poetry, and painting; and he occupied his leisure during his confinement in executing beautiful miniatures and paintings upon glass, after the manner of those times. Some of these paintings remained in the window of a church in Dijon, where they were placed soon after René painted them, for several hundred years.

It has already been stated that the name by which Margaret's father is commonly designated is King René. The origin of this royal title is now to be explained. He had an older brother, who became by inheritance, with Joanna his wife, king and queen of the Two Sicilies, that is, of the kingdom consisting of the island of Sicily and the territory connected with Naples on the main land. The brother, at the close of his life, designated René as his heir. This happened in the year 1436, while René was still in captivity in the castle of Dijon. He could, of course, do nothing himself to assert his claims to this new inheritance, but Isabella immediately assumed the title of Queen of the Two Sicilies for herself, and began at once to make preparation for proceeding to Italy and taking possession of the kingdom.

While maturing her plans, she took up her residence for a time at the chateau of Tarascon, on the banks of the Rhone, with the two children who remained under her care, namely, her son Louis and Margaret. Her other son was at Dijon with his father, and the other daughter, Yolante, had been given up, as has already been said, to the custody of the wife of Antoine, with a view of being married, as soon as she was old enough, to Antoine's son.

The children attracted great, attention at Tarascon. Their mother Isabella was by birth a lady of very high rank, her family being intimately connected with the royal family of France. She was now, too, by title at least, herself a queen. The children were very intelligent and beautiful, and the misfortunes and cruel captivity of their father and brother were known and talked of in all the country around. So the peasants and their families crowded around the chateau to see the children.

They brought them wreaths of flowers and other votive offerings. They sang songs to serenade them, and they built bonfires around the walls of the chateau at night, to drive away the infection of the plague, which was then prevailing in some parts of the country, and was exciting considerable alarm.

The people of the country believed that this plague was produced by magic and witchcraft, and there were some poor old women, who came with the other peasants to the walls of the chateau of Tarascon to see the children, who were believed to be witches. Afterward the plague broke out at Tarascon, and Margaret's mother was obliged to go away, taking the children with her. The poor women were, however, seized and burned at the stake, it being universally believed that it was they who had caused the plague.

Isabella's arrangements were now so far matured that she went at once into Italy with the children, and took up her abode there in the town of Capua. René still remained in captivity, but Isabella caused him to be proclaimed King of the Two Sicilies with great pomp and parade. At the time of this ceremony, the two children, Margaret and her brother, were seated beside their mother in a grand state carriage, which was lined with velvet and embroidered with gold, and in this way they were conveyed through the streets of the city.

After a time René was liberated from his confinement, and restored to his family, but he did not long enjoy this apparent return of prosperity. His claim to the kingdom of Naples was disputed, and, after a conflict, he was expelled from the country. In the mean time, the English had so far extended their conquests in France that both his native province of Anjou, and his wife's inheritances in Lorraine, had fallen into their hands, so that with all the aristocratic distinction of their descent, and the grandeur of their royal titles, the family were now, as it were, without house or home. They returned to France, and Isabella, with the children, found refuge from time to time with one and another of the great families to which she was related, while René led a wandering life, being reduced often to a state of great destitution.

He, however, bore his misfortunes with a very placid temper, and amused himself, wherever he was, with music, poetry, and painting. He was so cheerful and good-natured withal that he made himself a very agreeable companion, and was generally welcome, as a visitor, wherever he went. He retained the name of King René as long as he lived, though he was a king without a kingdom.

At one time he was reduced, it is said, to such straits that to warm himself he used to walk to and fro in the streets of Marseilles, on the sunny side of the buildings, which circumstance gave rise to a proverb long known and often quoted in those parts, which designated the act of going out into the sun to escape from the cold as warming one's self at King René's fireside.

Such was the family from which Margaret of Anjou sprung.

5

Royal Courtship

WHEN Margaret was not more than fourteen or fifteen years of age, she began to be very celebrated for her beauty and accomplishments, and for the charming vivacity of her conversation and her demeanor. She resided with her mother in different families in Lorraine and in other parts of France, and was sometimes at the court of the Queen of France, who was her near relative. All who knew her were charmed with her. She was considered equally remarkable for her talents and for her beauty. The arrangement which had been made in her childhood for marrying her to the Count of St. Pol was broken off, but several other offers were made to her mother for her hand, though none of them was accepted. Isabella was very proud of her daughter, and she cherished very lofty aspirations in respect to her future destiny. She was therefore not at all inclined to be in haste in respect to making arrangements for her marriage.

In the mean time, the feud between the uncles and relatives of King Henry, in England, as related in a preceding chapter, had been going on, and was now reaching a climax. The leaders of the two rival parties were, as will be recollected, Henry Beaufort, Bishop of Winchester, or Cardinal Beaufort, as he was more commonly called, who had had the personal charge of the king during his minority, on one side, and the Duke of Gloucester, Henry's uncle, who had been regent of England during the same period, on the other. The king himself was now about twenty-four years of age, and if he had been a man of vigor and resolution, he might perhaps have controlled the angry disputants, and by taking the government fully into his own hands, have forced them to live together in peace under his paramount authority. But Henry was a very timid and feeble-minded man. The turbulence and impetuousness of his uncles and their partisans in their quarrel was altogether too great for any control that he could hope to exercise over them. Indeed, the great question with them was which should contrive the means of exercising the greatest control over him.

In order to accomplish this end, both parties began very early to plan and manoeuvre with a view of choosing the king a wife. Whichever of the two great leaders should succeed in negotiating the marriage of the king, they knew well would, by that very act, establish his influence at court in the most absolute manner.

Princes and kings in those days, as, indeed, is the case to a considerable extent now, had some peculiar difficulties to contend with in making their matrimonial arrangements, so far at least as concerned the indulgence of any personal preferences which they might themselves entertain on the subject. Indeed, these arrangements were generally made for them, while they were too young to have any voice or to take any part in the question, and nothing was left for them but to ratify and carry into effect, when they came to years of maturity, what their parents, or grand councils of state, had determined for them when they were children, or else to refuse to ratify and confirm it at the cost of incurring a vast amount of difficulty and political entanglement, and perhaps even open and formidable war.

And even in those cases where the prince or king arrived at an age to judge for himself before any arrangements were made for him, which was the fact in regard to Henry VI., he was still very much embarrassed and circumscribed in his choice if he attempted to select a wife for himself. He could not visit foreign courts and see the princesses there, so as to judge for himself who would best please him; for in those days it was very unsafe for personages of any considerable rank or position to visit foreign countries at all, except at the head of an army, and in a military campaign. In the case, too, of any actually reigning monarch, there was a special difficulty in the way of his leaving his kingdom, on account of the feuds and quarrels which always in such cases arose in making the necessary arrangements for the government of the kingdom during his absence.

For these and various other causes, a king or a prince desiring to choose a wife was obliged to content himself with such information relating to the several candidates as he could obtain from hearsay in respect to their characters, and from miniatures and portraits in respect to their personal attractions. This was especially the case with King Henry VI. Each of the two great parties, that of Cardinal Beaufort on one hand, and that of the Duke of Gloucester on the other, were desirous of being the means of finding a bride for the king, and both were eagerly looking in all directions, and plotting for the accomplishment of this end, and any attempt of the king to leave the kingdom for any purpose whatever would undoubtedly have brought these parties at once to open war.

The Duke of Gloucester and those who acted with him fixed their eyes upon three princesses of a certain great family, called the house of Armagnac. Their plan was to open negotiations with this house, and to obtain portraits of the three princesses, to be sent to England, in order that Henry might take his choice of them. Commissioners were appointed to manage the business. They were to open the negotiations and obtain the portraits. The cardinal, of course, and his friends were greatly interested in preventing the success of this plan, though, of course, it was necessary for them to be discreet and cautious in manifesting any open opposition to it in the then present stage of the affair.

The king was very particular in the instructions which he gave to the commissioners in respect to the portraits, with a view of securing, if possible, perfectly correct and fair representations of the originals. He wished that the princesses should not be flattered at all by the artist in his delineation of them, and that they should not be dressed at their sittings in any unusually elegant manner. On the contrary, they were to be painted "in their kirtles simple, and their visages like as ye see, and their stature, and their beauty, and the color of their skin, and their countenances, just as they really are." The artist was instructed, too, by the commissioners to be expeditious in finishing the pictures and sending them to England, in order that the king might see them as soon as possible, and make his choice between the three young ladies whose "images" were to be thus laid before him.

This plan for giving the king an opportunity to choose between the three princesses of Armagnac, nicely arranged as it was in all its details, failed of being carried successfully into effect; for the father of these princesses, as it happened, was at this same time engaged in some negotiations with the King of France in respect to the marriage of his daughters, and he wished to keep the negotiations with Henry in suspense until he had ascertained whether he could or could not do better in that quarter. So he contrived means to interrupt and retard the work of the artist, in order to delay for a time the finishing of the pictures.

In the mean time, while the Duke of Gloucester and his party were thus engaged in forwarding their scheme of inducing Henry to make choice of one of these three princesses for his wife, the cardinal himself was not idle. He had heard of the beautiful and accomplished Margaret of Anjou, and, after full inquiry and reflection, he determined in his own mind to make her his candidate for the honor of being Queen of England. The manner in which he contrived to introduce the subject first to the notice of the king was this.

There was a certain man, named Champchevrier, who had been taken prisoner in Anjou in the course of the wars between France and England, and who was now held for ransom by the knight who had captured him. He was not, however, kept in close confinement, but was allowed to go at large in England on his parole—that is, on his word of honor that he would not make his escape and go back to his native land until his ransom was paid.

Now this Champchevrier, though a prisoner, was a gentleman by birth and education; and while he remained in England, held by his parole, was admitted to the best society there, and he often appeared at court, and frequently held converse with the king. In one of these interviews he described, in very glowing terms, the beauty and remarkable intelligence of Margaret of Anjou. It is supposed that he was induced to this by Cardinal Beaufort, who knew of his acquaintance with Margaret, and who contrived the interviews between Champchevrier and the king, in order to give the former an opportunity to speak of the lady to his majesty incidentally, as it were, and in a way not to excite the king's suspicions that the commendations of her which he heard were prompted by any match-making schemes formed for him by his courtiers.

If this was the secret plan of the cardinal, it succeeded admirably well. The king's curiosity was strongly awakened by the piquant accounts that Champchevrier gave him of the brilliancy of young Margaret's beauty, and of her charming vivacity and wit.

"I should like very much to see a picture of the young lady," said the king.

"I can easily obtain a picture of her for your majesty," replied Champchevrier, "if your majesty will commission me to go to Lorraine for the purpose."

Champchevrier considered that a commission from the king to go to Lorraine on business for his majesty would be a sufficient release for him from the obligations of his parole.

The king finally gave Champchevrier the required authority to leave the kingdom. Champchevrier was not satisfied with a verbal permission merely, but required the king to give him a regular safe-conduct, drawn up in due form, and signed by the king's name. Having received this document, Champchevrier left London and set out upon his journey, the nature and object of the expedition being of course kept a profound secret.

A certain nobleman, however, named the Earl of Suffolk, was admitted to the confidence of the king in this affair, and was by him associated with Champchevrier in the arrangements which were to be made for carrying the plan into execution. It would seem that he accompanied Champchevrier in his journey to Lorraine, where Margaret was then residing with her mother, and there assisted him in making arrangements for the painting of the picture. They employed one of the first artists in France for this purpose. When the work was finished, Champchevrier set out with it on his return to England.

In the mean time, the English knight whose prisoner Champchevrier was, heard in some way that his captive had left England, and had returned to France, and the intelligence made him exceedingly angry. He thought that Champchevrier had broken his parole and had gone home without paying his ransom. Such an act as this was regarded as extremely dishonorable in those days, and it was, moreover, not only considered dishonorable in a prisoner himself to break his parole, but also in any one else to aid or abet him in so doing, or to harbor or protect him after his escape. The knight determined, therefore, that he would at once communicate with the King of France on the subject, explaining the circumstances, and asking him to rearrest the supposed fugitive and send him back.

So he went to the Duke of Gloucester, and, stating the case to him, asked his grace to write to the King of France, informing him that Champchevrier had escaped from his parole, and asking him not to give him refuge, but to seize and send him back. Gloucester was very willing to do this. It is probable that he knew that Champchevrier was a friend of the cardinal's, or at least that he was attached to his interests, and that it was altogether probable that his going into France was connected with some plot or scheme by which the cardinal and his party were to derive some advantage. So he wrote the letter, and it was at once sent to the King of France. The King of France at this time was Charles VII.

The king, on receiving the letter, gave orders immediately that Champchevrier should be arrested. By this time, however, the painting was finished, and Champchevrier was on the way with it from Lorraine toward England. He was intercepted on his journey, taken to Vincennes, and there brought before King Charles, and called upon to give an account of himself.

Of course he was now obliged to tell the whole story. He said that he had not broken his parole at all, nor intended in any manner to defraud his captor in England of the ransom money that was due to him, but had come to France by the orders of the King of England. He explained, too, what he had come for, and showed Charles the painting which he was carrying back to the king. He also, in proof of the truth of what he said, produced the safe-conduct which King Henry had given him.

King Charles laughed very heartily at hearing this explanation, and at perceiving how neatly he had discovered the secret of King Henry's love affairs. He was much pleased, too, with the idea of King Henry's taking a fancy to a lady so nearly related to the royal family of France. He thought that he might make the negotiation of such a marriage the occasion for making peace with England on favorable terms. So he dismissed Champchevrier at once, and recommended to him to proceed to England as soon as possible, and there to do all in his power to induce King Henry to choose Margaret for his queen.

Champchevrier accordingly returned to England and reported the result of his mission. The king was very much pleased with the painting, and he immediately determined to send Champchevrier again to Lorraine on a secret mission to Margaret's mother. He first, however, determined to release Champchevrier entirely from his parole, and so he paid the ransom himself for which he had been held. The Duke of Gloucester watched all these proceedings with a very jealous eye. When he found that Champchevrier, on his return to England, came at once to the king's court, and that there he held frequent conferences, which were full of mystery, with the king and with the cardinal, and when, moreover, he learned that the king had paid the ransom money due to the knight, and that Champchevrier was to be sent away again, he at once suspected what was going on, and the whole court was soon in a great ferment of excitement in respect to the proposed marriage of the king to Margaret of Anjou.

The Duke of Gloucester and his party were, of course, strongly opposed to Margaret of Anjou; for they knew well that, as she had been brought to the king's notice by the other party, her becoming Queen of England would well-nigh destroy their hopes and expectations for all time to come. The other party acted as decidedly and vigorously in favor of the marriage. There followed a long contest, in which there was plotting and counterplotting on one side and on the other, and manoeuvres without end. At last the friends of the beautiful little Margaret carried the day; and in the year 1444 commissioners were formally appointed by the governments of England and France to meet at the city of Tours at a specified day, to negotiate a truce between the two countries preparatory to a permanent peace, the basis and cement of which was to be the marriage of King Henry with Margaret of Anjou. The truce was made for two years, so as to allow full time to arrange all the details both for a peace between the two countries, and also in respect to the terms and conditions of the marriage.

As soon as the news that this truce was made arrived in England it produced great excitement. The Duke of Gloucester and those who were, with him, interested to prevent the accomplishment of the marriage, formed a powerful political party to oppose it. They did not, however, openly object to the marriage itself, thinking that not politic, but directed their hostility chiefly against the plan of making peace with France just at the time, they said, when the glory of the English arms and the progress of the English power in that country were at their height. It was very discreditable to the advisers of the king, they said, that they should counsel him to stop short in the career of conquest which his armies were pursuing, and thus sacrifice the grand advantages for the realm of England which were just within reach.

The discussions and dissensions which arose in the court and in Parliament on this subject were very violent; but in the end Cardinal Beaufort and his party were successful, and the king appointed the Earl of Suffolk embassador extraordinary to the court of France to negotiate the terms and conditions of the permanent peace which was to be made between the two countries, and also of the marriage of the king. At first Suffolk was very unwilling to undertake this embassy. He feared that, in order to carry out the king's wishes, he should be obliged to make such important concessions to France that, at some future time, when perhaps the party of the Duke of Gloucester should come into power, he might be held responsible for the measure, and be tried and condemned, perhaps, for high treason, in having been the means of sacrificing the interests and honor of the kingdom by advising and negotiating a dishonorable peace. These fears of his were probably increased by the intensity of the excitement which he perceived in the Gloucester party, and perhaps, also, by open threats and demonstrations which they may have uttered for the express purpose of intimidating him.

At any rate, after receiving the appointment, his courage failed him, and he begged the king to excuse him from performing so dangerous a commission. The king was, however, very unwilling to do so. Finally, it was agreed that the king should give the earl his written order, executed in due and solemn form, and signed with the great seal, commanding him, on the royal authority, to undertake the embassage. Suffolk relied on this document as his means of defense from all legal responsibility for his action in case his enemies should at any future time have it in their power to bring him to trial for it.

In negotiating the peace, and in arranging the terms and conditions of the marriage, a great many difficulties were found to be in the way, but they were all, at last overcome. One of these difficulties was made by King René, the father of Margaret. He declared that he could not consent to give his daughter in marriage to the King of England unless the king would first restore to him and to his family the province of Anjou, which had been the possession of his ancestors, but which King Henry's armies had overrun and conquered. The Earl of Suffolk was very unwilling to cede back this territory, for he knew very well that nothing would be so unpopular in England, or so likely to increase the hostility of the

English people to the proposed marriage, and consequently to give new life and vigor to the Gloucester party in their opposition to it, as the giving up again of territory which the English troops had won by so many hard-fought battles and the sacrifice of so many lives. But René was inflexible, and Suffolk finally yielded, and so Anjou was restored to its former possessors.

Another objection which René made was that his fortune was not sufficient to enable him to endow his daughter properly for so splendid a marriage; not having the means, he said, of sending her in a suitable manner into England.

But this the King of England said should make no difference. All that he asked was the hand of the princess without any dowry. Her personal charms and mental endowments were sufficient to outweigh all the riches in the world; and if her royal father and mother would grant her to King Henry as his bride, he would not ask to receive with her "either penny or farthing."

King Henry was made all the more eager to close the negotiations for the marriage as soon as possible, and to consent to almost any terms which the King of France and René might exact, from the fact that there was a young prince of the house of Burgundy—a very brave, handsome, and accomplished man—who was also a suitor for Margaret's hand, and was very devotedly attached to her. This young prince was in France at this time, and ready, at any moment, to take advantage of any difficulty which might arise in the negotiations with Henry to press his claims, and, perhaps, to carry off the prize. Which of the two candidates Margaret herself would have preferred there is no means of knowing. She was yet only about fifteen years of age, and was completely in the power and at the disposal of her father and mother. And then the political and family interests which were at stake in the decision of the question were too vast to allow of the personal preferences of the young girl herself being taken much into the account.

At last every thing was arranged, and Suffolk returned to England, bringing with him the treaty of peace and the contract of marriage, to be ratified by the king's council and by Parliament. A new contest now ensued between the Gloucester and Beaufort parties. The king, of course, threw all his influence on the cardinal's side, and so the treaty and the contract carried the day. Both were ratified. The Earl of Suffolk, as a reward for his services, was made a marquis, and he was appointed the king's proxy to proceed to France and espouse the bride in the king's name, according to the usual custom in the case of royal marriages.

6

The Wedding

PREPARATIONS were now immediately made for solemnizing the marriage and bringing the young queen at once to England. The marriage ceremony by which a foreign princess was united to a reigning prince, according to the custom of those times, was two-fold, or, rather, there were two distinct ceremonies to be performed, in one of which the bride, at her father's own court, was united to her future husband by proxy, and in the second the nuptials were celebrated anew with her husband himself in person, after her arrival in his kingdom. Suffolk, as was stated in the last chapter, was appointed to act as the king's proxy in this case, for the performance of the first of these ceremonies. He was to proceed to France, espouse the bride in the king's name, and convey her to England. Of course a universal excitement now spread itself among all the nobility and among all the ladies of the court, which was awakened by the interest which all took in the approaching wedding, and the desire they felt to accompany the expedition.

A great many of the lords and ladies began to make preparations to join Lord and Lady Suffolk. Nothing was talked of but dresses, equipments, presents, invitations, and every body was occupied in the collecting and packing of stores and baggage for a long journey. At length the appointed time arrived, and the expedition set out, and, after a journey of many days, the several parties which composed it arrived at Nancy, the capital city of Lorraine, where the ceremony was to be performed.

At about the same time, the King and Queen of France, accompanied by a great concourse of nobles and gentlemen from the French court, who were to honor the wedding with their presence, arrived. A great many other knights and ladies, too, from the provinces and castles of the surrounding country, were seen coming in gay and splendid cavalcades to the town, when the appointed day drew nigh, eager to witness the ceremony, and to join in the magnificent festivities which they well knew would be arranged to commemorate and honor the occasion. In a word, the whole town became one brilliant scene of gayety, life, and excitement.

The marriage ceremony was performed in the church, with great pomp and parade, and in the midst of a vast concourse of people, composed of the highest nobility of Europe, both lords and ladies, and all dressed in the most magnificent and distinguished costumes. No spectacle could possibly be more splendid and gay. At the close of the ceremony, the bride was placed solemnly in charge of Lady Suffolk, who was to be responsible for her safety and welfare until she should arrive in England, and there be delivered into the hands of her husband. Lady Suffolk was a cousin of Cardinal Beaufort, and she undoubtedly received this very exalted appointment through his favor. The appointment brought with it a great deal of patronage and influence, for a regular and extended household was now to be organized for the service of the new queen, and of course, among all the lords and ladies who had come from England, there was a very eager competition to obtain places in it. There are enumerated among those who were appointed to posts of service or honor in attendance on the queen, under the Marchioness of Suffolk, five barons and baronesses, seventeen knights, sixty-five squires, and no less than one hundred and seventy-four valets, besides many other servitors, all under pay. Then, in addition to these, so great was the eagerness to occupy some recognized station in the train of the bride, that great numbers applied for appointments to nominal offices for which they were to receive no pay.

If René, Margaret's father, had been possessed of a fortune corresponding to his rank, the expense of all these arrangements, at least up to the time of the departure of the bridal party, would have been defrayed by him; but as it was, every thing was paid for by King Henry, and the precise amount of every expenditure stands recorded in certain old books of accounts which still remain among the ancient English archives.

The nuptials of the princess were celebrated by a tournament and other accompanying festivities, which were continued for eight days. In these tournaments a great many mock combats were fought, in which the most exalted personages present on the occasion took conspicuous and prominent parts. The King of France himself appeared in the lists, and fought with René, the father of the bride. The king was beaten. It would have been impolite for any one to have vanquished the father of the bride at a tournament held in honor of the daughter's nuptials. The Count St. Pol, too, who had formerly been betrothed to Margaret, but had not been allowed to marry her, fought very successfully, and won a valuable prize, which was conferred upon him with great ceremony by the hands of the two most distinguished ladies present, namely, the Queen of France and Isabella of Lorraine, the bride's mother. Perhaps he too was politely allowed to win his victory and his honorary prize, in consideration of his submitting so quietly to the loss of the real prize which his great competitor, the King of England, was so triumphantly bearing away from him.

The celebrations of the eight days were interrupted and enlivened by one remarkable incident, which for a time threatened to produce very serious difficulty. It will be remembered that when the original contract and treaty were made between René and the uncle of Isabella, Antoine of Vaudemonte, at the time when peace was re-established between them, after the battle in which René was taken prisoner, that not only was it agreed that Margaret should be betrothed to the Count St. Pol, but also that Yolante, Margaret's elder sister, was betrothed to Antoine's son Ferry, as he was called. Now Ferry seemed not disposed to submit quietly, as St. Pol had done, to the loss of his bride, and as he had never thus far been able to induce René and Isabella to fulfill their agreement by consenting to the consummation of the marriage, he determined now to take the matter into his own hands. So he formed the scheme of an elopement. His plan was to take advantage of the excitement and confusion attendant on the tournament for carrying off his bride. He organized a band of adventurous young knights who were willing to aid him in his enterprise, and, laying his plans secretly and carefully, he, assisted by his comrades, seized the young lady and galloped away with her to a place of safety, intending to keep her there in his own custody until King René and her mother should consent to her immediate marriage, King René, when he first heard of his daughter's abduction, was very angry, and declared that he would never forgive either Ferry or Yolante. But the King and Queen of France interceded for the lovers, and René at last relented. Ferry and Yolante were married, and all parties were made friends again, after which the celebrations and festivities were renewed with greater spirit and ardor than before.

At length the time for the conclusion of the public rejoicings at Nancy, and for the commencement of Margaret's journey to England, arrived. Thus far, though nominally under the care and keeping of Lord and Lady Suffolk, Margaret had of course been really most intimately associated with her own family and friends; but now the time had come when she was to take a final leave of her father and mother, and of all whom she had known and loved from infancy, and be put really and fully into the trust and keeping of strangers, to be taken by them to a distant and foreign land. The parting was very painful. It seems that Margaret's beauty and the charming vivacity of her manners had made her universally beloved, and the hearts not only of her father and mother, but of the whole circle of those who had known her, were filled with grief at the thought of parting with her forever.

The King and Queen of France, who seem to have loved their niece with sincere affection, determined to accompany her for a short distance, as she set out on her journey from Nancy. Of course, many of the courtiers went too. These, together with the great number of English nobles and gentry that were attached to the service of the bride, made so large a company, and the dresses, caparisons, and trappings which were exhibited on the occasion were so splendid and fine, that the cavalcade, as it set out from the city of Nancy on the morning when the journey was to commence, formed one of the gayest and grandest bridal processions that the world has ever seen.

After proceeding for five or six miles the procession came to a halt, in order that the King and Queen of France might take their leave. The parting filled the hearts of their majesties with grief. The king clasped Margaret again and again in his arms when he bade her farewell, and told her that in placing her, as he had done, upon one of the greatest thrones in Europe, it seemed to him, after all, that he had really done nothing for her, "for even such a throne is scarcely worthy of you, my darling child," said he. In saying this his eyes filled with tears. The queen was so overwhelmed with emotion that she could not speak; but, kissing Margaret again and again amid her sobbings and tears, she finally turned from her and was borne away.

Margaret's father and mother did not take their leave of her at this place, but went on with her two days' journey, as far as to the town of Bar le Duc, which was near the frontiers of Lorraine. Here they, too, at last took their leave, though their hearts were so full, when the moment of final parting came that they could not speak, but bade their child farewell with tears and caresses, unaccompanied with any words whatever of farewell.

Still Margaret was not left entirely alone among strangers when her father and mother left her. One of her brothers, and some other friends, were to accompany her to England. She had, moreover, by this time become well acquainted with the Marquis and Marchioness of Suffolk, under whose charge and protection she was now traveling, and she had become strongly attached to them. They were both considerably advanced in life, and were grave and quiet in their demeanor, but they were very kind and attentive to Margaret in every respect, and they made every effort in their power to console the grief that she felt at parting with her parents and friends, and leaving her native land, and they endeavored in every way to make the journey as comfortable and as agreeable as possible to her.

During all this time a vessel, which had been dispatched from England for the purpose, was waiting at a certain port on the northern coast of France called Kiddelaws, ready to take the queen and her bridal train across the Channel. The distance from Nancy to this port was very considerable, and the means and facilities for traveling enjoyed in those days were so imperfect that a great deal of time was necessarily employed on the journey. Besides this, a long delay was occasioned by the want of funds. King Henry had himself agreed to defray all the expenses of the marriage, and also of the progress of the bridal party through France to England. These expenses were necessarily great, and it happened at this time that the king was in very straitened circumstances in respect to funds. He was greatly embarrassed, too, in the efforts which he made to procure money, by the difficulties which were thrown in his way by the party of the Duke of Gloucester, who resisted by every means in their power all action of Parliament tending to furnish the king's treasury with money, and thus promote the final accomplishment of the marriage.

In consequence of all these difficulties and delays, it was nearly three months from the time when the bridal ceremony was performed at Nancy before Margaret was ready to embark for England in the vessel that awaited her at Kiddelaws.

It was not merely for the expenses of the journey through France of Margaret and her train that Henry had to provide. On her arrival in England there was to be a grand reception, which would require many costly equipages, and the giving of many entertainments. Then, moreover, the marriage ceremony was to be performed anew, and in a far more pompous and imposing manner than before, and after the marriage a coronation, with all the attendant festivities and celebrations. All these things involved great expense, and Margaret could not come into the kingdom until the preparations were made for the whole. To such straits was the king reduced in his efforts to raise the money which he deemed necessary for the proper reception of his bride, that he was obliged to pledge a large portion of the crown jewels, and also of the family plate and other personal property of that kind. A considerable part of the property so pledged was never redeemed.

At length, however, things were so far in readiness that orders arrived for the sailing of the expedition. The party accordingly embarked, and the vessel sailed. They crossed the Channel, and entered Portsmouth harbor, and finally landed at the town of Porchester, which is situated at the head of the harbor. The voyage was not very agreeable. The vessel was small, and the Channel in this place is wide, and Margaret was so sick during the passage, and became so entirely exhausted, that when the vessel reached the port she could not stand, and Suffolk carried her to the shore in his arms.

The boisterous weather which had attended the party during their voyage increased till it ended in a dreadful storm of thunder, lightning, and rain, which burst over the town of Porchester just at the time while the party were landing. The people, however, paid no attention to the storm and rain, but flocked in crowds into the streets where the bride was to pass, and strewed rushes along the way to make a carpet for her. They also filled the air with joyful acclamations as the procession passed along. In this way the royal bride was conveyed through the town to a convent in the vicinity, where she was to rest for the first night, and prepare for continuing her journey to London.

The next day, the weather having become settled and fair, it was arranged that Margaret and her party should be conveyed from Porchester to Southampton along the shore in barges. The water of this passage is smooth, being sheltered every where by the land. The barges first moved down Portsmouth harbor, then out into what is called the Solent Sea, which is a narrow, sheltered, and beautiful sheet of water, lying between the Isle of Wight and the main land, and thence, entering Southampton Water, they passed up, a distance of eight or ten miles, to the town.

On the arrival of the queen at Southampton, she was conveyed again to a convent in the vicinity of the town, for this was before the days of hotels. Here she was met by persons sent from the king to assist her in respect to her farther preparations for appearing at his court. Among other measures that were adopted, one was the sending a special messenger to London to bring an English dressmaker to Southampton, in order that suitable dresses might be prepared for the bride, to enable her to appear properly in the presence of the English ladies at the approaching ceremonies.

In the mean time, King Henry, whom the rules of royal etiquette did not allow to join the queen until the time should arrive for the performance of the second part of the nuptial ceremony, came down from London, and took up his abode at a place ten or twelve miles distant, called Southwick, where he had a palace and a park. The nuptials were to be celebrated at a certain abbey called Lichfield Abbey, which was situated about midway between Southampton, where the queen was lodged, and Southwick, the place of waiting for the king. The king had expected that every thing would be ready in a few days, but he was destined to encounter a new delay. Margaret had scarcely arrived in Southampton when she was attacked by an eruptive fever of some sort, resembling small-pox, which threw all her friends into a state of great alarm concerning her. The disease, however, proved less serious than was at first apprehended, and after a week or two the danger seemed to be over.

During all the time while his bride was thus sick Henry remained in great suspense and anxiety at Southwick, being forbidden, by the rigid rules of royal etiquette, to see her.

At length Margaret recovered, and the day was appointed for the final celebration of the nuptials. When the time arrived, Margaret was conveyed in great state, and at the head of a splendid cavalcade, to the abbey, and there the marriage ceremony was again performed in the presence of a great concourse of lords and ladies that had come from

London and Windsor, or from their various castles in the country around, to be present on the occasion.

Suffolk Presenting Margaret to the King

This final ceremony was performed in April, 1445. Of course, as Margaret was born in March, 1429, she was at this time sixteen years and one month old.

Among other curious incidents which are recorded in connection with this wedding, there is an account of Margaret's receiving, as a present on the occasion—for a pet, as it were, just as at the present day a young bride might receive a gift of a spaniel or a canary-bird—a lion. It was very common in those times for the wealthy nobles to keep such animals as these at their castles. They were confined in dens constructed for them near the castle walls. The kings of England, however, kept their lions, when they had any, in the Tower of London, and the practice thus established of keeping wild beasts in the Tower was continued down to a very late period; so that I remember of often reading, when I was a boy, in English story-books, accounts of children, when they went to London, being taken by their parents to see the "lions in the Tower."

Margaret sent her lion to the Tower. In the book of expenses which was kept for this famous bridal progress, there is an account of the sum of money paid to two men for taking care of this lion, feeding him and conveying him to London. The amount was £2 5s. 3d., which is equal to about ten or twelve dollars of our money. This seems very little for such a service, but it must be remembered that the value of money was much greater in those times than it is now.

Immediately after the marriage ceremony was completed, the preparations for the journey having been all made beforehand, the king and queen set out together for London, and it soon began to appear that this part of the journey was to be more splendid and gay than any other. The people of the country, who had heard marvelous stories of the youth and beauty and the early family misfortunes of the queen, flocked in crowds along the roadsides to get a glimpse of her as she passed, and to gaze on the grand train of knights and nobles that accompanied her, and to admire the magnificence of the dresses and decorations which were so profusely displayed. Every body came wearing a daisy in his cap or in his button-hole, for the daisy was the flower which Margaret had chosen for her emblem. At every town through which the bride passed she was met by immense crowds that thronged all the accessible places, and filled the windows, and in some places covered the roofs of the houses and the tops of the walls, and welcomed her with the sound of trumpets, the waving of banners, and with prolonged shouts and acclamations.

In the mean time, the Duke of Gloucester, who, with his party, had done every thing in his power to oppose the marriage, now, finding that it was an accomplished fact, and that all farther opposition would not only be useless, but would only tend to hasten and complete his own utter downfall, concluded to change his course, and join heartily himself in the general welcome which was given to the bride. His plan was to persuade the queen that the opposition which he had made to King Henry's measures was directed only against the peace which had been made with France, and which he had opposed for political considerations alone, but that, so far as the marriage with Margaret was concerned, he approved it. So he prepared to outdo, if possible, all the rest of the nobility in the magnificence of the welcome which he was to give her on her arrival in London. He possessed a palace at Greenwich, on the Thames, a short distance below London, and he sent an invitation to Margaret to come there on the last day of her journey, in order to rest and refresh herself a little preparatory to the excitement and fatigue of entering London. Margaret accepted this invitation, and when the bridal procession began to draw nigh, Gloucester came forth to meet her at the head of a band of five hundred of his own retainers, all dressed in his uniform, and wearing the badge of his personal service. This great parade was intended partly to do honor to the bride, and partly to impress her with a proper sense of his own rank and importance as one of the nobles of England, and of the danger that she would incur in making him her enemy.

Very splendid preparations were made in the city of London to do honor to the royal bride in her passage through the city. It was the custom in those times to exhibit in the streets, on great public days, tableaux, and emblematic or dramatic representations of certain truths or moral sentiments appropriate to the occasion, and sometimes of passages of Scripture history. A great many of these exhibitions were arranged by the citizens of London, to be seen by the bride and the bridal procession as they passed through the streets. Some of these were very quaint and queer, and would only be laughed at at the present day. For instance, in one place was an arrangement of two figures, one dressed to represent justice, and the other peace; and these figures were made movable and fitted with strings, so that, at the proper moment, when the queen was passing, they could be made to come together and apparently kiss each other. This was intended as an expression of the text, justice and peace have kissed each other, which was considered as an appropriate text to characterize and commemorate the peace between England and France which this marriage had sealed. In another place there was an emblematical pageant representing peace and plenty.

There were also, at other places, representations of Noah's ark, of the parable of the wise and foolish virgins, of the heavenly Jerusalem, and even one of the general resurrection and judgment day.

On the morning of the day appointed for the queen's entry into London, the pageants having all been prepared and set up in their places, a grand procession of the mayor and aldermen, and other dignitaries, was formed, and proceeded down the river toward Greenwich, in order to meet the queen and escort her through the city. These civic officers were all mounted on horseback, and dressed in their gay official costumes. The chiefs were dressed in scarlet, and the body of their followers, arranged in bands according to their respective trades, wore blue gowns, with embroidered sleeves and red hoods. In this way the royal procession was escorted over London Bridge, and through the principal streets of the city to Westminster, where the bride was at length safely received in the palace of her husband.

This was on the 28th of May. Two days afterward Margaret was crowned queen in Westminster with great parade and ceremony. The coronation was followed by a grand tournament of three days' duration, accompanied with banquets and other festivities usual on such occasions, and then at length the bride had the satisfaction of feeling that the long-protracted ceremony was over, and that she was now to be left to repose.

7

Reception in England

NOTWITHSTANDING the grand reception which the Duke of Gloucester gave to Margaret on her arrival in England, she knew very well that he had always been opposed to her marriage, and had not failed to do all in his power to prevent it. She accordingly considered him as her enemy; and though she endeavored at first, at least, to treat him with outward politeness, she felt a secret resentment against him in heart, and would have been very glad to have joined his political enemies in effecting his overthrow.

Cardinal Beaufort and the Earl of Suffolk, as has already been said, were Gloucester's rivals and enemies. The cardinal was a venerable man, now quite advanced in years. He was, however, extremely ambitious. He was immensely wealthy, and his wealth gave him great influence. He had, moreover, been the guardian of the king during his minority, and in that capacity had acquired a great influence over his mind. The Earl of Suffolk, who, with his lady, had been sent to France to bring Margaret over, had inspired Margaret with a great friendship for him. She felt a strong affection for him, and also for Lady Suffolk, not only on account of their having acted so important a part in promoting her marriage, but also on account of the very kind and attentive manner in which they had treated her during the whole period of her journey. Thus the cardinal and Suffolk, on the one hand, had the advantage, in their quarrel with the Duke of Gloucester, of great personal influence over the king and queen, while, Gloucester himself, on the other hand, enjoyed in some respects a still greater advantage in his popularity with the mass of the people. Every body perceived that the old quarrel between these great personages would now, on the arrival of the queen in England, be prosecuted with more violence than ever, and all the courtiers were anxious to find out which was likely to be the victor, so that, at the end of the battle, they might be found on the winning side.

As soon as the coronation was over, the principal personages who had been sent with Margaret by her father, for the purpose of accompanying her on her journey, and seeing her properly and comfortably established in her new home, were dismissed and allowed to set out on their return. They all received presents in money from King Henry to reimburse them for the expenses of the journey which they had made in bringing him his bride.

Margaret was thus left to herself in the new station and new sphere of duty to which she had been transferred. All the royal palaces had been fitted up expressly for her reception. This was very necessary in fact, for some years had elapsed since there had been a queen in England, and all the royal residences had become very much out of repair. Those were rude times, and even the palaces and castles that were built for kings and queens were at best very comfortless dwellings. But when,

Ancient Portrait of Queen Margaret

during a long minority, they were abandoned to the rude tenants and rough usages to which at such times they were sure to be devoted, they came, in the end, to be little better than so many barracks for soldiery. It required a great deal of time, and no little expense, to prepare the

Tower and the palaces of Westminster and Richmond for the reception of a young and beautiful queen, and of the gay company of ladies that were to attend her. King Henry was so destitute of money at this time that he found it extremely difficult to provide the means of paying the workmen. There is still extant a petition which the clerk of the works sent in to the king, praying him to supply him with more money to pay the men, for the labor was so poorly paid, and the wages were so much in arrears, that it was extremely difficult for him to find men, he said, to go on with the work.

The palaces were, however, at last made ready before Margaret came. There were apartments for her in the Tower, and there were also three other palaces in and near London, in either of which she could reside at her pleasure. Besides this, the cardinal, who, as has already been remarked, was possessed of immense wealth, owned, among his other establishments, a beautiful mansion at Waltham Forest, a few miles north of London. The cardinal set apart a state chamber in this house for the exclusive use of the queen when she came to visit him, and caused it to be fitted up and furnished in a magnificent manner for her. The drapery of the bed was of cloth of gold from Damascus, and the other furniture and fittings were to correspond. The queen used often to go and visit the cardinal at this country seat. She soon became very fond of him, and willing to be guided by his counsel in almost every thing that she did. Indeed, the ascendency which the cardinal thus exercised over Margaret greatly increased his power over the king. The affairs of the court and of the government were directed almost wholly by his counsels. The Duke of Gloucester and the nobles of his party became more and more indignant and angry al this state of things. The realm of England, they said, through the weakness and imbecility of the king, had fallen into the hands of a priest and of a woman—a French woman, too.

But there was nothing that they could do. Margaret was so young and so beautiful that every body was captivated with her person and behavior, and whatever she did was thought to be right. Indeed, the general course which she pursued on her first arrival in England was right in an eminent degree. There have been many cases in which young queens, in coming as Margaret did, away from their native land and from all their early friends, to reign in a foreign court, have brought with them from home personages of distinction to be their favorites and friends in their new position. But when this is done, jealousies and ill-will always sooner or later spring up between these relatives and friends of the foreign bride and the old native advisers of the king her husband. The result is, in the end, a king's party and a queen's party at court, and perpetual quarrels and dissensions ensue, in which at least the people of the country are sure to become involved, from their natural jealousy of the foreign influence, as they call it, introduced by the queen.

Queen Margaret had the good sense to avoid this danger. All the principal persons who came with her to England, for the purpose of accompanying her on the journey, and of carrying back to her father and friends in France authentic assurances of her having been honorably received by her husband as his bride and queen, were dismissed and sent home again immediately after the coronation, as we have already seen. Margaret retained only certain domestic servants, and perhaps some two or three private and personal friends. As for counselors and advisers, she threw herself at once upon the ministers and counselors of the king—the Cardinal Beaufort, who had been his guardian from childhood, and the Earl of Suffolk, who was one of his principal ministers, and had been sent by him, as his proxy and representative, to negotiate the marriage and bring home the bride. She made Lady Suffolk, too—the wife of the earl—her most intimate female friend. She appointed her to the principal place of honor in her household, and in other ways manifested great affection for her. The good sense and discretion which she thus manifested—young as she was, for she was not yet seventeen—in choosing for her confidential friend a lady of the age and standing of Lady Suffolk, instead of attempting to place in that position some foreign belle of her own years, whom she had brought with her for the purpose from her native land, as many young brides in her situation would have done, deserves much commendation. In a word, Margaret, in becoming a wife, gave herself up entirely to her husband. She made his friends her friends, and his interests her interests, and thus transferred herself, wholly and without reserve, to her new position; an example which all young ladies whose marriage brings them into entirely new circumstances and relations would do well to follow. Nothing is more dangerous than the attempt in such cases to bring from the old home influences in any form to be introduced with a view of sharing the control in the new.

In consequence of the discreet course of conduct that Margaret thus pursued, and of the effect produced on the court by her beauty, her vivacity, and her many polite accomplishments, public opinion—that is, the opinion of the outside world, who knew nothing of her secret designs or of her real character—turned very soon after her arrival in England entirely in her favor. As has already been said, the general sentiment of the nobles and of the people was strongly against the match when it was first proposed. They opposed it, not because they had any personal objection to Margaret herself, but because, in order to prepare the way for it, it was necessary to make peace with France, and in making peace, to grant certain concessions which they thought would weaken the power f of the English on the Continent, and, at any rate, greatly interfere with the farther extension of their power there. But when the people came to see and know the queen, they all admired and loved her.

As for the king, he was perfectly enchanted with his bride. He was himself, as has already been said, of a very sedate and quiet turn of mind; amiable and gentle in disposition; devout, fond of retirement, and interested only in such occupations and pleasures as are consistent with a life of tranquillity and repose. Margaret was as different as possible from all this. Her brilliant personal charms, her wit, her spirit, her general intellectual superiority, the extraordinary courage for which she afterward became so celebrated, and which began to show itself even at this early period, all combined to awaken in Henry's mind a profound admiration for his wife, and gave her a great and rapidly-increasing ascendency over him.

The impression which Margaret made upon the people was equally favorable. England, they thought, had never seen a queen more worthy of the throne than Margaret of Anjou. Some one said of her that no woman equaled her in beauty, and few men surpassed her in courage and energy. It seemed as if she had been born in order to supply to her royal husband the qualities which he required in order to become a great king.

8

The Story of Lady Neville

IN reading the history of the English monarchy in these early times, you will often hear of the court intrigues which mingled with, and sometimes greatly complicated, the movement of public affairs. Margaret of Anjou found herself, on her arrival in England, involved in many such intrigues. Indeed, she was admirably qualified, by her sagacity and quickness of apprehension, and by the great ascendency which these and other qualities which she possessed gave her over the minds of all about her, to take a very active and successful part in the management of manoeuverings of all sorts. The nature of these court intrigues is very well illustrated by the narration which the most celebrated of Margaret's biographers gives of one in which he says that Margaret herself became involved while on her way from France to England. The story seems much more like romance than like reality. Indeed, it doubtless is a romance, but it nevertheless illustrates well the manner in which the private passions and personal and family quarrels of the great became involved with, and sometimes entirely controlled, the most important events in the national history, and therefore it will not be amiss to relate it.

The first connection which Queen Margaret, as we are henceforth to call her, had with the affair of Lady Neville, took place at Abbeville, a town in France not very far from Calais, when the queen was advancing toward the sea-coast on her way to England. While she was at Abbeville, there suddenly appeared a young and beautiful lady who asked an audience of Margaret, announcing herself simply as one of the ladies who had been attached to the service of the dauphiness, who was the wife of the oldest son of the king, and who had recently died. She was admitted. She remained in private conversation with Margaret two hours, and when this mysterious interview was concluded she was introduced to the other ladies of Margaret's court as Miss Sanders, an English lady who had been attached to the court of the dauphiness, but who now, since the death of her mistress, wished to return to England in Margaret's train. Margaret informed the other ladies that she had received her into her household, and gave directions that she should be treated with the utmost consideration.

The other ladies were very curious to solve the mystery of this case, but they could not obtain any clew to it. The stranger was very reserved; mingled very little with her new companions, and evinced a constant desire to avoid observation. There was something, however, in her beauty, and in the expression of deep and constant grief which her countenance wore, which made her an object of great interest to all the household of the queen, but they could not learn any particulars of her history. The facts, however, were these.

Her real name was Anne Neville. She was the daughter of Richard Neville, Earl of Salisbury, one of the leading and most highly-connected noblemen in England. When she was about fifteen years old she was married to a relative of the family. The marriage, however, proved a very unhappy one. Her husband was very jealous of her. From her subsequent conduct it would seem probable that he might have had good reason to be so. At any rate, he was extremely jealous; and as he was of a harsh and cruel temper, he made his young wife very miserable by the exactions and privations which he enforced upon her, and by the violent invectives with which he continually assailed her.

The incessant anxiety and suffering which these troubles occasioned soon began to prey upon the lady's health, and, at length, her father, observing that she was growing pale and thin, began to inquire into the cause. He soon learned what a dreadful life his daughter was leading. Like most of the other great nobles of those days, he was a man of violent character, and he immediately determined on rescuing his daughter from her husband's power, for he considered her husband as the party chiefly, if not wholly, to blame.

He ascertained, or pretended to ascertain, that there had been some informalities connected with the marriage. His daughter was distantly related to her husband, and there were certain steps which it was necessary to take in such cases to obtain a dispensation from the Church, in order to render such marriage legal. These steps he now alleged had not been properly taken, and he immediately instituted proceedings to have the marriage annulled. Whether there was really any sufficient ground for such annulling, or whether he obtained the decree through influences which his high position enabled him to bring to bear upon the court, I do not know. He, however, succeeded in his purpose. The marriage was annulled, and his daughter returned home; and, in order to obliterate as far as possible all traces of the unhappy union into which she had been drawn, she dropped the name which she had received from her husband and resumed again her own maiden name.

She now began soon to appear at court, where she almost immediately attracted great attention. On account of the peculiar circumstances in which she was placed, she enjoyed all the privileges of a widow, combined with the attractiveness and the charms of a lovely girl. Almost every body was ready to fall in love with her.

Among her other admirers was the Duke of Somerset. He was a man of high rank and of great accomplishments, but he was married, and he could not, therefore, innocently make her the object of his love. He was not, however, deterred by this consideration, and he soon succeeded in making a strong impression upon Lady Neville's heart. They soon contrived means of meeting each other in private, resorting to all sorts of manoeuvres and inventions to aid them in keeping their guilty attachment to each other from the knowledge of those around them.

In the mean while, the Duke of Gloucester himself, who was now, however, considerably advanced in life, lost his wife, she dying about this time, and he almost immediately conceived the idea of making Lady Neville her successor. He thought it not proper to say any thing to Lady Neville herself on this subject until some little time should have elapsed, but he spoke to her father, the Earl of Salisbury, who readily approved of the plan. Gloucester was at this time prime minister of England, and the lady whom he should choose for his wife would be elevated by her marriage to the highest pinnacle of grandeur. Of course, the importance and influence of her father also, and of all the members of her family, would be greatly increased by so splendid an alliance.

So it was agreed that the match should be made, but the arrangement was to be kept secret, not only from the public, but from the intended bride herself; until a suitable time should have elapsed for the widower to recover from the grief which the death of his former wife was supposed to have occasioned him.

At length, when the proper time for mourning had expired, Gloucester made his declaration of love. Lady Neville listened to it, thinking all the time what Somerset would say when she came to communicate the news to him. She did communicate it to him on the first opportunity.

Great was the distress and the perplexity which the lovers felt while consulting together and determining what was to be done in such an emergency. They could not endure the thought of a separation. They could not be married to each other, for Somerset was married already. For Lady Neville to remain single all her life in order to be at liberty to indulge a guilty passion was an idea not to be entertained. They knew, too, that their present relations to each other could not long be continued. A thousand circumstances might happen at any time to interrupt or to terminate it, and it could not be long, in any event, before it must come to an end. So it was agreed between them that Lady Neville should accede to the great minister's proposal and become his wife. In the mean time, until the period should arrive for the consummation of the marriage, they were to renew and redouble their intimacy with each other, taking, however, every possible precaution to conceal their movements from the eyes of others.

So the duke's offer was accepted, and it was soon made known to all the court that Lady Neville was his affianced bride.

Thus far Lady Neville had treated the duke with great reserve in her accidental intercourse with him at the reunions of the court, but now, since he was her accepted lover, he thought he might reasonably expect a greater degree of cordiality in her demeanor toward him. But he found no change. She continued as formal and reserved as ever. Moreover, when he went to visit her, which he did sometimes several times a day, she was very often not at home—much too often, he thought. He went to the place where her domestics said she had gone in such cases, but she was very seldom to be found. He soon came to the conclusion that there was some strange mystery involved in the affair, and he determined to adopt effectual measures for unraveling it.

So he employed certain trusty persons who were in his service to watch and see where Lady Neville went, and how she passed her time during these unaccountable absences from home. For many days this watch was continued, but no discoveries were made, The spies reported that they could not keep upon the lady's track. In spite of their best exertions she would contrive to elude them, and for several hours every day they lost sight of her altogether. They saw enough, however, to satisfy them that there was something wrong going on. What it was, however, they could not discover, so shrewd and complete were the precautions which Somerset and Lady Neville had taken to prevent detection.

The Duke of Gloucester was for a time much perplexed to know what to do, whether openly to quarrel with Lady Neville and refuse to consummate the marriage, or to banish his suspicions and take her for his wife. His love for her finally triumphed, and he resolved to proceed with the marriage. He had no positive evidence against her, he said to himself and then, besides, even if there were some secret attachment on her part, to account for these mysterious appearances, she might, after, all, when once married to him, make him a faithful and affectionate wife.

Some lingering remains of a former affection must often necessarily dwell, he thought, in the heart of a bride, even when truly and honestly giving herself to the one on whom her choice is finally made. Especially is this true in cases where the lady is young, accomplished, and lovely, while her husband can only offer wealth or high position instead of youth and personal attractions as a means of winning her favor.

So it was decided that the marriage should take place, and the day for the wedding was appointed.

When the time for the wedding drew nigh, and the lovers found that the period of their enjoyments was drawing to a close, they determined on having a farewell interview with each other on the day before the wedding, and in order to be safe from interruption, it was arranged that they should spend the day together in a village on the banks of the Thames, at some little distance from London.

When the day came, Lady Neville left her home to repair to the place of rendezvous. She was followed by Gloucester's spies. She was received at the village by Somerset. Somerset was, however, so disguised that the spies did not know and could not discover who he was. They were satisfied, however, from his demeanor toward Lady Neville, that he was her lover, and they at once reported the facts to Gloucester in London.

Gloucester was of course in a great rage. He swore terrible vengeance against both Lady Neville herself and her lover, whoever he might be. He at once armed a troop of his followers and rode off at the head of them, guided by one of the spies, to the village of rendezvous. It was dark before he arrived there. Some peasants of whom he made inquiry informed him that a lady answering to the description which he gave them had gone on board the boat to return to London some time before. Gloucester immediately turned, and made all haste back to London again, in hopes to reach the landing before the boat should arrive, with a full determination to kill both the lady herself and her paramour the moment they should touch the shore.

He was mistaken, however, in supposing that the paramour, whoever he might be, was with the lady. Somerset, in the excess of his precaution, had returned to London by land, leaving Lady Neville to return by herself in the boat with the other passengers; for the boat was a sort of packet which plied regularly between the village and London. He, however, had stationed trusty persons not far from the landing in London, who were to receive Lady Neville on her arrival and convey her home.

Gloucester arrived at the landing before the boat reached the shore. It was, however, now so dark that he despaired of being able to recognize the persons he was in pursuit of, especially under the disguise which he did not doubt that they would wear. So, in the recklessness of his rage, he resolved to kill every body in the boat, and thus to make sure of his revenge.

Accordingly, the moment that the boat touched the shore, he and his followers rushed on board and a dreadful scene of consternation and terror ensued. Gloucester himself made his way directly toward the figure of a lady, whose air, and manner, and style of dress indicated, so far as he could discern them in the darkness, that she was probably the object of his fury. He plunged his dagger into her breast. She, in an agony of terror, leaped into the river. She was buoyed up by her dress, and floated down the stream.

In the mean time, the work of murder on board the boat went on. The duke and his men continued stabbing and striking down all around them, until the passengers and the boat-men were every one killed. The bodies were then all thrown into the river, stones having been previously tied to them to make them sink.

The people in the houses of the neighborhood, on the banks of the river, heard the cries, and raised their heads a moment from their pillows, or paused as they were walking along the silent streets to listen. But the cries were soon suppressed, for the massacre was the work of a few moments only, and such sounds were far too common in those days in the streets of London, and especially on the river, to attract much regard.

The boat was of course covered with blood. The duke ordered his men to take it out into the middle of the river and sink it, that being the easiest and the quickest way of covering up all traces and proofs of the crime.

The writer who relates this story says that Gloucester's reason for wishing to have his agency in this transaction concealed was not that he feared any punishment, for the laws in those days were wholly powerless to punish deeds of violence like this, committed by men of Gloucester's rank and station. He only thought that if it were known that he had murdered in this way so many innocent people, in order merely to make sure of killing an object of his own private jealousy and hate, it would injure his popularity!

In the mean tithe, Lady Neville, for it was really Lady Neville whom Gloucester had stabbed, and who had leaped into the river, floated on down the stream, borne up by her dress, which was made, according to the fashion of the times, in a manner to give it great buoyancy in the water, by means of the hoops with which the sleeves of the robe were distended, and also from the form of the head-dress, which was very large and light, and well adapted to serve as a float to keep the head from sinking.

She floated on in this manner down the river until she had passed London Bridge, being carried through by the current under on of the arches. On emerging from the bridge, she came to the part of the river where the ships and other vessels bound down the river were moored. It happened that among other vessels lying at anchor in the stream was one bound to Normandy. The captain of this vessel had been on shore, but he was now coming off in his boat to go on board again. As the captain was looking out over the water by the light of a lantern which he held in his hand, to discern the way to his vessel, he saw something floating at a short distance from him which resembled the dress of a woman. He urged the boat forward in that direction. He succeeded, with great difficulty, after arriving at the spot, in getting the now almost lifeless form of Lady Neville on board his boat, and then rowed on as fast as possible to the vessel.

Female Costume in the Time of Henry VI

Here every thing was done which the case required to restore the drowning lady to life. She soon recovered her senses, and looked about her wild with excitement and terror. She had the presence of mind, however, not to say a word that could betray her secret, though her dress, and her air and manner, convinced the captain that she was no ordinary personage. The wound was examined and found not to be serious. She had been protected by some portions of her dress which had turned the poniard aside. When she found that the immediate danger had passed she became more composed, and began to inquire in regard to the persons and scenes around her. When she found that the vessel which had received her was bound to Normandy, she determined to escape to that country; so she contrived means to induce the captain to conceal her on board until the time should arrive for setting sail, and then to take her with him down the river and across the Channel.

On her arrival in France she repaired at once to the court of the dauphiness, who, being an English princess, was predisposed to take compassion upon her and to receive her kindly. She remained at this court, as we have seen, under the assumed name of Miss Sanders, until the death of the dauphiness. She was thus suddenly deprived of her protector in France, but almost at the same time the marriage of Margaret of Anjou seemed to open to her the means of returning to England.

So long as the Duke of Gloucester lived and retained his power, she knew very well that she could not return in safety to the English court; but she thought that Margaret's going to England, would probably be the precursor of Gloucester's downfall.

"She must hate him," said she to herself, "almost as much as I do, for he has opposed her marriage from the beginning, and has done all in his power to prevent it. Margaret will never be satisfied until she has deposed him from his power and put some friend of hers in his place. I can help her in this work, if she will receive me under her protection and allow me to accompany her to England."

So she proceeded to Abbeville to intercept the queen on her way to the coast, as we have already seen. At the long and secret interview which she had with her there she related to Margaret the story of her connection with Somerset and with Gloucester, and of her almost miraculous escape from death at Gloucester's hands. She now wished for revenge; and if Queen Margaret would receive her into her service and take her to England, she would concert measures with Somerset, her lover, which would greatly aid Margaret in the plans which she might form for effecting the downfall of Gloucester.

Margaret at once and very gladly acceded to this request, and took Lady Neville with her to England. She treated her with great consideration and honor; but still Lady Neville maintained a strict reserve in all her intercourse with the other ladies of the court, and kept herself in great seclusion, especially after the arrival of the bridal party in England. Her pretext for this was her deep affliction at the loss of her friend and patroness the Dauphiness of France. But the other ladies of the court were not wholly satisfied with this explanation. They were fully convinced that there was more in the case than met the view, especially when they found that on the arrival of the party in England the stranger seemed to take special pains to avoid meeting the Duke of Gloucester. They exerted all their powers of watchfulness and scrutiny to unravel the mystery, but in vain.

9

Plottings

IT was in this way that public affairs were mingled and complicated with private and personal intrigues in the English court at the time of Margaret's arrival in the country. Margaret was of a character which admirably fitted her to act her part well in the management of such intrigues, and in playing off the passions of ambition, love, resentment, envy, and hate, as manifested by those around her—passions which always glow and rage with greater fury in a court than in any other community—so as to accomplish her ends. She was very young indeed, but she had arrived at a maturity, both mental and personal, far beyond her years. Her countenance was beautiful, and her air and manner possessed an inexpressible charm, but her mental powers were of a very masculine character, and in the boldness of the plans which she formed, and in the mingled shrewdness and energy with which she went on to the execution of them, she evinced less the qualities of a woman than of a man.

It was supposed by all parties in England that Lady Neville was dead. Of course the Duke of Gloucester had no idea that any one could have escaped from the boat. He supposed that he had effected the complete destruction of all on board of it. Somerset's men, who had been stationed at some distance from the landing to receive Lady Neville and convey her home, waited until long past the appointed hour, but no one came. The inquiries which Somerset made secretly the next day showed that the boat had sailed from the village, but no tidings of her arrival in London could be obtained, and he supposed that she must have been lost, with all on board, by some accident on the river. As for the Earl of Salisbury, Lady Neville's father, Gloucester went to him at once, and informed him what he had done. He had detected his daughter, he said, in a guilty intrigue, which, if it had been made public, would have brought not only herself, but all her family, to shame. The earl, who was a man of great sternness and severity of character, said that Gloucester had done perfectly right, and they agreed together to keep the whole transaction secret from the world, and to circulate a report that Lady Neville had died from some natural cause.

Such was the state of things when Margaret and Lady Neville arrived in London. As soon as the queen became somewhat established in her new home, she began to revolve in her mind the means of deposing Gloucester. Her plan was first to endeavor to arouse her husband from his lethargy, and to awaken in his mind something like a spirit of independence and a feeling of ambition.

"You have in your hands," she used to say to him, "what may be easily made the foundation of the noblest realm in Europe. Besides Great Britain, you have the whole of Normandy, and other valuable possessions in France, which together form a vast kingdom, the government of which you might acquire great glory, if you would take the government of it into your own hands."

She went on to represent to him how unworthy it was of him to allow all the power of such a realm to be wielded by his uncle, instead of assuming the command at once himself, as every consideration of prudence and policy urged him to do. A great many instances had occurred in English history, she said, in which a favorite minister had been allowed to hold power so long, and to strengthen himself in the possession of it so completely, that he could not be divested of it, so that the king himself came at length to be held in subjection by his own minister. The Duke of Gloucester was advancing rapidly in the same course; and, unless the king aroused himself from his inaction, and took the government into his own hands, he would soon lose all power to do it, and would sink into a condition of humiliating dependence upon one of his own subjects.

Then, again, she urged upon him at other times the example of his father and grandfather, Henry IV. and Henry V., whose reigns, through the personal energy and prowess which they had exhibited in strengthening and extending their dominions, had given them a world-wide renown. It would be extremely inglorious for the descendant of such a line to spend his life in spiritless inactivity, and to leave the affairs of his kingdom in the hands of a relative, who of course could only be expected to exercise his powers for the purpose of promoting his own interest and glory.

Moreover, she reminded him of a danger that he was in from the representations of other branches of the royal line who still claimed the throne, and might at any time, whenever an opportunity offered, be expected to attempt to enforce their claims. As will be seen by the genealogical table, Lionel, the second son of Edward III.—whose immediate descendants had been superseded by those of John of Gaunt, the third son, on account of the fact that the only child of Lionel was a daughter, and she had been unable to make good her claims—had a great-granddaughter, named Anne, who married Richard, a son of Edmund, the fourth of the sons of Edward III.

Richard Plantagenet, who issued from this union, was, of course, the descendant and heir of Lionel. He had also other claims to the throne, and Margaret reminded her husband that there was danger at any time that he might come forward and assert his claims.

Under these circumstances, it was evident, said she, that the king could not consider his interests safe in the care of any person whatsoever out of his own immediate family—that is, in any one's hands but his own and those of his wife. A minister, however strong his professions of fidelity and attachment might be, could not be depended upon. If another dynasty offered him more advantageous terms, there was not, and there could not be, any security against his changing sides; whereas a wife, whose interests were bound up inseparably with those of her husband, might be relied upon with absolute certainty to be faithful and true to her husband in every conceivable emergency.

These representations which Margaret made to her husband from time to time, as she had opportunity, produced a very considerable impression upon him. Still he seemed not to have resolution and energy enough to act in accordance with them. He said that he did not see how he could take away from his uncle a power which he had always exercised well and faithfully. And then, besides, he himself had not the age and experience necessary for the successful management of the affairs of so mighty a kingdom. If he were to undertake the duties of government, he was convinced that he should make mistakes, and so get into difficulty. Margaret, however, clearly perceived that she was making progress in producing an impression upon her husband's mind. To increase the influence of her representations, she watched for occasions in which Gloucester differed in opinion from the king, and failed to carry out suggestions or recommendations which the king had made, relating probably, in most cases, to appointments to office about the court. Some say she created these occasions by artfully inducing her husband to make recommendations which she knew the duke would not sanction. At all events, such cases occurred, and Margaret took advantage of them to urge her views still more upon Henry's mind.

"How humiliating," said she, "that a great monarch should be dependent upon one of his subjects for permission to do this or that, when he might have all his affairs under his own absolute control!"

But Henry, in reply to this, said that it was not in human nature to escape mistakes, and he thought he was very fortunate in having a minister who, when he was in danger of making them, could interpose and save him from the ill consequences which would otherwise result from his errors.

To this Margaret rejoined that it was indeed true that human nature was liable to err, but that it was very humiliating for a great and powerful sovereign to have public attention called to his errors by having them corrected in that manner by an inferior, and to be restricted in the exercise of his powers by a tutor and a governor, in order to keep him from doing wrong, as if he were a child not competent to act for himself.

"Besides," she added, "if you would really take the charge of your affairs into your own hands and act independently, what you call your errors you may depend upon it the public would designate by a different and a softer name. The world is always disposed to consider what is done by a great and powerful monarch as of course right, and even when it would seem to them wrong they believe that its having that appearance is only because they are not in a position to form a just judgment on the question, not being fully acquainted with the facts, or not seeing all the bearings of them."

She assured her husband, moreover, that if he would take the business of the government into his own hands, he would be very successful in his administration of public affairs, and would be well sustained by all the people of the realm.

Besides thus operating upon the mind of the king, Margaret was secretly employed all the time in ascertaining the views and feelings of the principal nobles and other great personages of the realm, with a view to learning who were disposed to feel hostile to the duke, and to unite all such into an organized opposition to him. One of the first persons to whom she applied with this view was Somerset, the former lover of Lady Neville.

She presumed, of course, that Somerset would be predisposed to a feeling of hostility to the duke on account of the old rivalry which had existed between them, and she now proposed to make use of Lady Neville's return, and of her agency in restoring her to him, as a means of inducing him to enter fully into her plans for overturning his old rival's power. In order to retain the management of the affair wholly in her own hands, she agreed with Lady Neville that Lady Neville herself was not in any way to communicate with Somerset until she, the queen, had first had an interview with him, and that he was to learn the safety of Lady Neville only through her. Lady Neville readily consented to this, believing that the queen could manage the matter better than she herself could do it.

It will be recollected that Somerset was married during the period of his former acquaintance with Lady Neville, but his wife had died while Lady Neville was in France, and he was now free; so that the plan which the queen and lady Neville now formed was to give him an opportunity, if he still retained his love for her, to make her his wife.

In the prosecution of her design, the queen made arrangements for a secret interview with Somerset, and in the interview informed him that Lady Neville was still alive and well; that she was, moreover, not far away, and it was in the queen's power to restore her to him if he desired again to see her, and that she would do so on certain conditions.

Somerset was overjoyed at hearing this news. At first he could not be persuaded that it was true; and when assured positively that it was so, and that the long lost Lady Neville was alive and well, and in England, he was in a fever of impatience to see her again. He would agree to any conditions, he said, that the queen might name, as the price of having her restored to him. The queen said that the conditions were three.

The first was that he was to see her but once, and that only for a few minutes, in order that he might be convinced that she was really alive, and then was to leave her and not to see her again until the Duke of Gloucester had fallen from power.

The second was that he should pretend to be not on good terms with the queen herself, in order to avert suspicion in respect to some of her schemes until such time as she should be ready to receive him again into favor.

The third was that he should do all he could to increase and strengthen the party against the duke, by turning as many as possible of his friends, and those over whom he had any influence, against him, and then finally, when the party should become sufficiently strong, to prefer charges against him in Parliament, and bring him to trial.

Somerset at once agreed to all these conditions, and the queen then admitted him to an interview with Lady Neville.

He was overwhelmed with transports of love and joy at once more beholding her and pressing her in his arms. The queen, who was present, was very much interested in witnessing the proofs of the ardor of the affection by which the lovers were still bound to each other, but she soon interrupted their expressions and demonstrations of delight by calling Somerset's attention to the steps which were next to be taken to further their plans.

"The first thing to be done," said she, "is for you to see the Earl of Salisbury and ask the hand of his daughter, and at the same time endeavor to induce him to join our party."

The Earl of Salisbury had a son, the brother, of course, of Lady Neville, whose title was the Earl of Warwick. He was the celebrated king-maker, so called, referred to in a former chapter. He received that title on account of the great influence which he subsequently exercised in raising up and putting down one after another of the two great dynasties. His power was at this time very great, partly on account of his immense wealth, and partly on account of his commanding personal character. Margaret was extremely desirous of bringing him over to her side.

Somerset readily undertook the duty of communicating with the Earl of Salisbury, with a view, of informing him of his daughter's safety and asking her hand, and at the same time of ascertaining what hope there might be of drawing him into the combination which the queen was forming against the Duke of Gloucester.

Somerset accordingly sought an interview with Salisbury, and told him that the report which had been circulated that his daughter was dead was not true—that she was still alive—that, instead of having been drowned in the Thames, as had been supposed, she had made her escape to France, where she had since lived under the protection of the dauphiness.

He was, of course, not willing to make known the real circumstances of the case in respect to the cause of her flight, and so he represented to the earl that the reason why she left the country was to escape the marriage with Gloucester, which would have been extremely disagreeable to her. She had now, however, returned, and he was commissioned by her to ask the earl's forgiveness for what had passed, and his consent that he himself—that is, Somerset, who had always been strongly attached to her, and who now, by the death of his former wife, was free, should be united to her in marriage.

If Somerset had succeeded in this part of his mission, he was then intending, when the old earl's love for his daughter should have been reawakened in his bosom by the joyful news that she was alive, and by the prospect of a brilliant marriage for her, to introduce the subject of the Duke of Gloucester, and perhaps cautiously reveal to him the true state of the case in respect to the murderous violence with which the duke had assailed his daughter, and which was the true cause of her flight. But the earl did not give him any opportunity to approach the second part of his commission. After having heard the statement which Somerset made to him in respect to his daughter, he broke out in a furious rage against her. He called her by the most opprobrious names. He had full proof of her dishonor, and he would have nothing more to do with her. He had disinherited her, and given all her share of the family property to her brother; and the only reason why he ever wished her to come into his sight again was that he might with a surer blow inflict upon her the punishment which Gloucester had designed for her.

Somerset saw at once that the case was hopeless, and he withdrew.

Thus the attempt to draw Salisbury into the conspiracy against the duke seemed for the time to fail. But Margaret was not at all discouraged. She pushed her manoeuvres and intrigues in other quarters with so much diligence and success that, in about two years after her arrival in England, she found her party large enough and strong enough for action.

10

The Fall of Gloucester

AT length the time arrived when Margaret considered her schemes ripe for execution.

Accordingly, one day, while Henry and herself were together in the king's cabinet engaged in transacting some public affairs, Margaret made some excuse for sending for Gloucester, and while Gloucester was in the cabinet, Somerset, according to a preconcerted arrangement, presented himself at the door with an air of excitement and alarm, and asked to be admitted. He wished to see the king on business of the utmost urgency. He was allowed to come in. He had a paper in his hand, and his countenance, as well as his air and manner, denoted great apprehension and anxiety. As soon, however, as he saw the Duke of Gloucester, he seemed surprised and embarrassed, and was about to retire, saying he had supposed that the king and queen were alone.

But Margaret would not allow him to withdraw.

"Stay," said she, "and let us know what the business is that seems so urgent. You can speak freely. There is no one here beside ourselves except the minister of the king, and there is nothing to be concealed from him."

Somerset, on hearing these words, paused for a moment, looked at Gloucester, seemed irresolute, and then, as if nerving himself to a great effort, he advanced resolutely and presented the paper which he had in his hands to the king, saying, at the same time, in a very solemn manner, that it contained charges of the gravest character against Gloucester; and he added that, on the whole, he was not sorry that the accused person was present to know what was laid to his charge, and to reply if he had any proper justification to offer.

The duke seemed thunderstruck. The king, too, was extremely surprised, and began to look greatly embarrassed. Margaret put an end to the awkward suspense by taking the paper from the king's hand, and opening it in order to read it.

"Let us see," said she, "what these charges are."

The Charges against Gloucester

So she opened the paper and began to read it. The charges were numerous. The principal one related to some transactions in respect to the English dominions on the Continent, in which Gloucester was accused of having sacrificed the rights and interests of the crown in order to promote certain private ends of his own. There were a great many other accusations, relating to alleged usurpations of the prerogative of the king and high-handed violations of the laws of the land. Among these last the murder of Lady Neville was specified, and the deed was characterized in the severest terms as a crime of the deepest dye, and one committed under circumstances of great atrocity, although the author of the charges admitted that the details of the affair were not fully known.

As Margaret read these accusations one after another, the duke affirmed positively of each one that it was wholly unjust. He seemed for a moment surprised and confused when the murder of Lady Neville was laid to his charge, but he soon recovered himself, and declared that he was innocent of this crime as well as of all the others. The whole series of accusations was a tissue of base calumnies, he said, from beginning to end.

Margaret read the paper through, parsing only from time to time to hear what Gloucester had to say whenever he manifested a desire to speak, but without making any observations of her own. She assumed, in fact, the air and manner of an unconcerned and indifferent witness. After she had finished reading the paper she folded it up and laid it aside, saying at the same time to the king that those were very grave and weighty charges, and it would be very unjust to the duke to receive them against his positive declarations of his innocence, without the most clear and conclusive proof.

"At the same time," she added, "they ought not to be lightly laid aside without investigation. We can not suppose that the Duke of Somerset can have made such charges without any evidence whatever to sustain them."

The Duke of Somerset said immediately that he was prepared with full proof of all the charges, and he was ready to offer the evidence in respect to any one or all of them whenever his majesty should require it.

Margaret then opened the paper, and, looking over the list of charges again with a careless air, at last, as if accidentally, fixed upon the one relating to the murder of Lady Neville.

"What proofs have you in respect to this atrocious murder that you have charged against the duke?"

Gloucester felt for the moment much relieved at finding that this was the charge selected first for proof; for so effectual had been the precautions which he had taken to conceal his crime in this case, that he was confident that, instead of any substantial evidence against him, there could be, at worst, only vague grounds of suspicion, and these he was confident he could easily show were insufficient to establish so serious a charge.

Somerset asked permission to retire for a few moments. Very soon he returned, bringing in with him Lady Neville herself. An actual resurrection from the dead could not have astounded Gloucester more than this apparition. He was overwhelmed with amazement and almost with terror. Lady Neville advanced to the king, and, falling upon her knees before him, she related the circumstances of the assault made by Gloucester upon the boat in the Thames, of the cruel murder of the passengers and boatmen, of the wound inflicted upon herself by the dagger of the duke, and the almost miraculous manner in which she made her escape.

The duke, overwhelmed by the emotions which such a scene might have been expected to produce upon his mind, seemed to admit that what Lady Neville said was true. At least he could not deny it, and his confusion and distress amounted apparently to a virtual confession of guilt. Margaret, however, soon interrupted the proceeding by saying to the king that the case was plainly too serious to be disposed of in so private and informal a manner. It was for the Parliament to consider it, she said, and decide what was to be done; and measures ought at once to be taken for bringing it before them.

So Gloucester and Somerset were both dismissed from the royal presence, leaving the king in a state of great distress and perplexity.

Such is the story of the private manoeuvres resorted to by Margaret with a view to destroying the hold which the Duke of Gloucester had upon the mind of the king, preparatory to more widely-extended plans for ruining him with the Parliament and the nation, which is told by one of her most celebrated biographers. Whether there was or was not any foundation for this particular story, there is no doubt but that she exercised all her ingenuity and talent as a manoeuvrer to accomplish her object, and that she succeeded. The king was brought over to her views, and so strong a party was formed against Gloucester among the nobles and other influential personages in the land, that at length, in 1447, a Parliament was summoned with a view of bringing the affair to a crisis.

Nothing, however, was said, in calling the Parliament, of the great and exciting business which was to be brought before them. So great was the power of such a man as Gloucester, that any open attempt to arrest him would have been likely to have been met with armed resistance, and might have led at once to civil war.

One of the charges against him was that he was intriguing with the Duke of York, the representative and heir of the two other branches of old King Edward the Third's family, who has already been mentioned as claiming the throne. It was said that Gloucester was secretly plotting with Richard, with a view of deposing Henry, and raising Richard to the throne in his stead.

The question of the succession was really, at this time, in a very curious state. The Duke of Gloucester himself was Henry's heir in case he should die without children; for Gloucester was Henry's oldest uncle, and, of course, in default of his descendants, the crown would go back to him. This was one reason, perhaps, why he had opposed Henry's marriage.

So long, therefore, as Henry remained unmarried, it was for Gloucester's interest to maintain the rights of his branch of the family—that is, the Lancaster line—against the claims of the house of York. But in case Henry should have children, then he would be cut off from the succession on the Lancaster side, and then it might be for his interest to espouse the cause of the house of York, provided he could make better terms in respect to his own position and the rewards which he was to receive for his services on that side than on the other.

Now Henry was married, and, moreover, it had long been evident to Gloucester that his own influence was fast declining. The scene in the king's cabinet, when Somerset brought those charges against him, must have greatly increased his fears in respect to the continuance of his power under Henry's government. Still, if it was true that he was contemplating making common cause with the Duke of York, he had not yet so far matured his plans as to make any open change in his course of conduct.

Accordingly, when the plan of calling a Parliament was determined by the king and Margaret, every effort was made to keep it a secret from the public that the case of Gloucester was to be brought before it. It was summoned on other pretexts. The place of meeting was not, as usual, at London, for Gloucester was so great a favorite with the people of London that it was thought that, if it were to be attempted to arrest him there, he would certainly resist and attempt to raise an insurrection.

The Parliament was accordingly summoned to meet at Bury St. Edmund's—a town situated about fifty or sixty miles to the northeast of London, where there was a celebrated abbey. The English Parliament was in those days, as it is, in fact, in theory now, nothing more nor less than a convocation of the leading personages of the realm, called by the king, in order that they might give the monarch their counsel or aid in any emergency that might arise, and he could call them to attend him at any place within the kingdom that he chose to designate.

While thus, by summoning Parliament to meet at Bury St. Edmund's, the queen's party placed themselves beyond the reach of the friends and adherents of Gloucester, who were very numerous in and around the capital, they took care to have a strong force there on their own side, ready to do whatever might be required of them.

When the appointed day arrived the Parliament assembled. It met in the abbey. The great dining-hall of the abbey, or the refectory, as it was called, the room in which the monks were accustomed to take their meals, was fitted up for their reception. On the first day some ordinary business was transacted, and on the second, suddenly, and without any previous warning, the duke was arrested by the public officer, who was attended and aided in this service by a strong force, and immediately taken away to the Tower.

This event, of course, produced great excitement. The news of it spread rapidly throughout the kingdom, and it awakened universal astonishment and alarm.

It was expected that charges would be immediately brought against him, and that he would be at once arraigned for trial. But the excitement which the affair had created was increased to a ten-fold degree by the tidings which ware circulated a few days afterward that he was dead. The story was that he was found dead one morning in his prison. People, however, were slow to believe this statement. They thought that he had been poisoned, or put to death in some other violent manner. The officers of the government declared that it was not so; and, in order to convince the people that the duke had died a natural death, they caused the body to be exposed to public view for several days before they allowed it to be interred, in order that all might see that it bore no marks of violence.

The people were, however, not satisfied. They thought that there were many ways by which death might be produced without leaving any outward indications of violence upon the person. They persisted in believing that their favorite had been murdered.

One account which was given of the mode of death was that Somerset went to visit him in his prison in the Tower, in order to see whether he could not come to some terms with him, but that Gloucester rejected his advances with so much pride and scorn that a furious altercation arose, in the course of which Somerset, with the assistance of men whom he had brought with him, strangled or suffocated the unhappy prisoner on his couch, and then, after arranging his limbs and closing his eyes, so as to give him the appearance of being in a state of slumber, his murderers went away and left him, to be found in that condition by the jailer when he should come to bring him his food.

11

The Fall of Suffolk

AFTER the death of the Duke of Gloucester, Queen Margaret was plunged in a perfect sea of plots, schemes, manoeuvres, and machinations of all sorts, which it would take a volume fully to unravel. This state of things continued for two years, during which time she became more and more involved in the difficulties and complications which surrounded her, until at last she found herself in very serious trouble. I can only here briefly allude to the more prominent sources of her perplexity.

In the first place, the people of England were very seriously displeased at the treatment which Gloucester had received. They would not believe that he died a natural death, and the impression gained ground very generally that the queen was the cause of his being murdered. They did not suppose that she literally ordered him to be put to death, but that she gave hints or intimations, as, royal personages were accustomed to do in such cases in those days, on which some zealous and unscrupulous follower ventured to act, certain of pleasing her. As Gloucester had been a general favorite with the nation, these rumors and suspicions tended greatly to alienate the hearts of the people from the queen. Many began to hate her. They called her the French woman, and vented their ill-will in obscure threats and mutterings.

This feeling of hostility to the queen was increased by the very unfortunate turn that things were taking in France about this time. The provinces of Maine and Anjou lay directly to the south of Normandy, which last was the most valuable of the possessions which the English crown held in France, and these two provinces had been given up to the French at the time of Margaret's marriage. It was only on condition that the English would give them up that Lord Suffolk could induce Margaret's father to consent to the match. Suffolk was extremely unwilling to surrender these provinces. He knew that the English nobles and people would be very much dissatisfied as soon as they learned that it was done, and he feared that he might at some future day be called to account for having been concerned in the transaction. But the king was so deeply in love with Margaret that he insisted on Suffolk's complying with the terms which were exacted by her friends, and the provinces were ceded.

The Duke of York was regent in France at that time, but Margaret felt some uneasiness in respect to his position there. He was the representative and heir of the rival line; and while it was for her interest to give him prominence enough under Henry's government to prevent his growing discontented and desperate, it was not good policy to exalt him to too high a position. She was accordingly somewhat at a loss to decide what to do.

Soon after the death of Gloucester, Somerset, finding that he was an object of suspicion, felt himself to be in danger, and he proposed to Margaret that he should retire into Normandy for a time. Margaret suggested that he should take the regency of Normandy in the Duke of York's stead. To this he finally consented. The Duke of York was recalled, and Somerset went to take command of Normandy in his stead.

At the time that Suffolk negotiated the marriage contract between Henry and Margaret, a truce had been made with the King of France, as has already been stated. Suffolk intended and hoped to conclude a permanent peace, but he could not succeed in accomplishing this. The King of France, as soon as the marriage was fairly carried into effect, seemed bent on renewing hostilities, and as he had now the territories of Maine and Anjou in his possession, with all the castles and fortresses which provinces contained, he could advance to the frontiers of Normandy on that side with facility, and organize expeditions for invading the country in the most effective manner.

He now only wanted a pretext, and a pretext in such cases is always soon found. A certain company of soldiers, who had been dismissed from some place in Maine in consequence of the cession of that province to France, instead of going across the frontier into Normandy to join the English forces there, as they ought to have done, went into Brittany, another French province near, and there organized themselves into a sort of band of robbers, and committed acts of plunder. The King of France complained of this to Somerset, for this was after Somerset had assumed the command as regent, or governor of Normandy. Somerset admitted the facts, and proposed to pay damages. The king named a sum so great that Somerset could not or would not pay it, and so war was again declared.

View of Rouen

In consequence of the advantages which the King of France enjoyed in having possession of Maine, he could organize his invading army in a very effective manner. He crossed the frontier in great force, and after taking a number of towns and castles, and defeating the English army in several battles, he at last drove Somerset into Rouen, the capital of the province—a very ancient and remarkable town—and shut him up there.

After a short siege Rouen was compelled to capitulate, and, besides giving up Rouen, Somerset was obliged to surrender several other important castles and towns in order to obtain his own liberty.

Things went on in this way during the year 1449, from bad to worse, until finally the whole of Normandy was lost. The town of Cherbourg, which has lately become so renowned on account of the immense naval and military works which have been constructed there, was the last retreat and refuge of the English, and even from this they were finally expelled.

The people of England were in a great rage. The principal object of their resentment was Lord Suffolk, who was now the first minister and the acknowledged head of the government. During the progress of the difficulties with Gloucester, Margaret had kept him a great deal in the background, in order that the public might not associate him with those transactions, nor hold him in any way responsible for them, though there was no doubt that he was the queen's confidential friend and counselor through the whole. After the death of Gloucester he had been gradually brought forward, and he had now, for some time, been the acknowledged minister of the crown, and as such responsible, according to the theory of the British Constitution and to the ideas of English- men, for every thing that was done, and especially for every thing like misfortune and disaster which occurred.

There was, of course, a great outcry raised against Suffolk, and also, more covertly, against the queen, who had brought Suffolk into power. All the mischief originated, too, people said, in the luckless marriage of Margaret to the king, and the cession of Maine and Anjou to the French as the price of it. The French would never have been able to have penetrated into Normandy had it not been for the advantage they gained in the possession of those provinces on the frontier.

View of Bordeaux

There were still large possessions held by the English in the southwestern part of France on the Garonne. The capital of this territory, which was the celebrated province of Guienne, was Bordeaux, a large and important city in those days as now. It stands on the bank of the river where it begins to widen toward the sea, and thus it was accessible to the English in their ships as well as when coming with their armies by land. It was a place of great strength as well as of commanding position, being provided with castles and towers to defend it from the landward side, and thick walls and powerful batteries along the margin of the water.

Suffolk did all in his power to raise and send off re-enforcements to the army in Guienne, but it was in vain. The English were driven out of one town and castle after another, until, at last, Bordeaux itself fell, and all was lost.

The resentment and rage of the people of England now knew no bounds. Suffolk was universally denounced as the author of all these dire calamities. Lampoons and satires were written against him; he was hooted sometimes by the populace of London when he appeared in the streets, and every thing portended a gathering storm. At length, in the fall of 1449, a Parliament was summoned. When it was convened, Suffolk appeared in the House of Lords as usual, and, rising in his place, he called the attention of the peers to the angry and vindictive denunciations which were daily heaped upon him by the public, declaring that he was wholly ignorant of the crimes which were laid to his charge, and challenging his enemies to bring forward any proof to sustain their accusations.

A spirit of bold defiance like this might have been successful in some cases, perhaps, in driving back the tide of hostility and hate which was rising so rapidly, but in this instance it seemed to have the contrary effect. The enemies of Suffolk in the House of Commons took up the challenge at once. They were strong enough to carry the house with them. They passed an address to the peers, requesting them to cause Suffolk to be arrested and imprisoned. They would, they said, immediately bring forward the proofs of his guilt.

The Lords replied that they could not arrest and imprison one of their number except upon specific charges made against him. Where upon the Commons very promptly prepared a list of charges and sent them to the Lords. On this accusation the Lords ordered Suffolk to be arrested, and he was sent to the Tower.

During the two months that succeeded his arrest his enemies were busily engaged in preparing the bill of impeachment against him in form, and collecting the evidence by which they were to sustain it, while the queen was equally earnest and anxious in the work of contriving means to save him. She visited him secretly, it is said, in his prison, and conferred with him on the plan to be pursued. They seem to have been both convinced that it was impossible for him to remain in England and ride out the storm. The only course of safety would be for him to leave the country for a while, provided the means could be devised of getting him away. What the plan was which they agreed upon for accomplishing this purpose will appear in the sequel.

At length, on the thirteenth of March; he was summoned before the House of Lords, and the bill of impeachment was brought forward. There were a great many charges, beginning with that of having wickedly and with corrupt motives surrendered, and so lost forever to the crown, the provinces of Maine and Anjou, and going on to numerous accusations of malfeasance in office; of encroachments on the prerogatives of the king, and of acts in which the interest and honor of the country had been sacrificed to his own personal ambition or private ends. Suffolk defended himself in a general speech, without, however, demanding, as he was entitled to do, a formal trial by his peers. These proceedings occupied several days—as long as any lingering hope remained in Suffolk's mind of his being able to stem the torrent. At length, however, on the seventeenth of March, finding that the pressure against him was continually increasing; and that there would be no chance of an acquittal if he were to claim a trial, he appealed to the king to decide his case, saying that, though he was entirely innocent of the crimes charged against him, he would submit himself entirely to his majesty's will.

In response to this appeal; the king declared, through the proper officer, in the House of Lords, that he would not decide upon the question of the guilt or innocence of the accused, since he had not demanded a trial, but he thought it best, under all the circumstances of the case, that Suffolk should leave the country. He therefore issued a decree of banishment against him for five years. He was required to leave England before the first of May, and not to put his foot upon any English soil until the five years were expired.

The Lords were much displeased at having the affair thus taken out of their hands. They made a formal protest against this decision, but they could do nothing more. The people, too, were very much enraged. They declared that Suffolk should never leave London alive; and on the day when they expected that he was to be taken from the Tower to be conveyed to France, a mob of two thousand men collected in the streets, resolved to kill him.

But the queen devised means for enabling him to evade them. Some of his servants and followers were seized, but he succeeded in making his escape, and; after going to his castle in the country, and making some hurried arrangements there, he went down to the sea-coast at Ipswich, a town in the eastern part of the island, and there embarked for France in a vessel which the queen had taken the precaution to have ready there for him.

The vessel immediately sailed, steering to the southward, of course, toward the Straits of Dover. As she was passing through the Straits, between Dover and Calais, a man-of-war named the Nicholas of the Tower, hove in sight, coming up to the vessel just as they were sending a boat on shore at Calais to inquire whether Suffolk would be allowed to land there. The boat was intercepted. At the same time, a boat from the man-of-war came on board the vessel, bringing officers who were instructed to search her thoroughly. Of course, they found Suffolk on board, and the officer, as soon as Suffolk was discovered, informed him that he must go with him on board the man-of-war.

Suffolk had no alternative but to obey. The captain of the man-of-war received him, as he stepped upon the deck, with the words, I am glad to see you, traitor, or something to that effect. Such a salutation must have plainly indicated to Suffolk what was before him. The man-of-war moved toward the English shore, and began to make signals to some parties on the land. She remained there for two days, exchanging signals in this way from time to time, and apparently awaiting orders.

At length, on the third day, a boat came off from the shore, provided with every thing that was necessary for the execution of a criminal. There was a platform with a block upon it, an axe, or cleaver of some sort, and an executioner. Suffolk was conveyed on board the boat, and there, with very little ceremony, his head was laid upon the block, and the executioner immediately commenced his task of severing it from the body. But, either from the unsteadiness of the boat, or the unsuitableness of the instrument, or the clumsiness of the operator, five several blows were required before the bloody deed was done.

The boat immediately proceeded to the shore. The men on board threw out the dissevered remains upon the beach, and then went away.

Some friends of Suffolk, hearing what had been done, came down to the beach, and, finding the separate portions of the body lying in the sand where they had been thrown, placed them reverently together again, and gave them honorable burial.

12

Birth of a Prince

AFTER the death of Suffolk the queen was plunged into a sea of anxious perplexities and troubles, which continued to disturb the kingdom and to agitate her mind, until at length, in 1453, eight or nine years after her marriage, she gave birth to a son. This event, strange as it may seem, aggravated the difficulties of her situation in a ten-fold degree.

The reason why the birth of her child increased her troubles was this. It has already been said that the Duke of York claimed to be the rightful sovereign of England on account of being descended from an older branch of the royal family; but that, since Henry was established upon the throne, he was inclined to make no attempt to assert his claims so long as it was understood that he was to receive the kingdom at Henry's death. In order to keep him contented in this position, it had been Margaret's policy to treat him with great consideration, and to bestow upon him high honors, but, at the same time, to watch him very closely, and to avoid conferring upon him any such substantial power within the realm of England as would enable him to attempt to seize the throne. She accordingly gave him the regency of France, and afterward, when she recalled him from that country in order to send Somerset there, she sent him to Ireland.

After the death of Suffolk, Somerset came home from France. Indeed, he was on his way home at the very time that Suffolk was killed, the English possessions there having been almost entirely lost. As soon as he returned, the queen received him into high favor at court, and soon made him the chief minister of the crown. The people of the country were displeased at this, and soon showed marks of great discontent. They would very likely have risen in open rebellion had it not been that Henry's health was so feeble, and the probability was so great that he would die without issue—in which case the crown would devolve peacefully to the Duke of York and his heirs.

"Let us wait," said they, "for a short time, and it will all come right. It is better to bear the evils of this state of things a little longer than to plunge the country into the horrors of civil war in attempting to change the dynasty by force before Henry dies."

In the mean time, however, although this was so far the prevailing public sentiment as to prevent an actual outbreak, it did not by any means save the community from being unnecessarily agitated by anxieties and fears lest an outbreak should take place, nor did it prevent innumerable plots and conspiracies being formed tending to produce one. The country was divided into two great parties—those that favored the Duke of York and his dynasty, and those who adhered to the house of Lancaster. The nobles took sides in the quarrel, some openly and others in secret. As these nobles were continually moving to and fro from one castle to another, or between the country and London, at the head of armed bodies of men more or less formidable, no one could tell what plans were being formed, or how soon an explosion might occur. The Duke of York was, of course, the head and leader of one side, and the Duke of Somerset, as the confidential counselor and minister of Henry and the queen, was the most prominent on the other side, and each of these great leaders regarded the other with feelings of mortal enmity.

This state of things kept both the king and queen in continual anxiety. The queen began to find that, by her manoeuvrings and management, she had involved herself in difficulties that were beyond her control, and the poor king was so harassed by his troubles and perplexities that his health, and, at last, his mind, began to suffer severely.

The Temple Garden

At length the Duke of York, without permission from the government, crossed the Channel from Ireland and landed in England. He soon collected a large armed force, and began to move across the country toward London. The government were much alarmed. He professed not to have any hostile object in view, and declared that he still acknowledged his allegiance to the Lancaster line; but there were no means of being sure that this was not a mere pretext, and that he might not, at any time, throw off his mask and rise in open rebellion.

It was about this time that the famous symbols of the red and the white rose were chosen as the badges of the houses respectively of York and Lancaster, as has already been mentioned. The story goes that at a certain time, while several nobles and persons of the court were walking in what is called the Temple Garden, a piece of open and ornamental ground on the bank of the river in London, Somerset and Warwick, who were on different sides in this quarrel, gathered, the one a white, and the other a red rose, and proposed to the rest of the company to pluck roses too, each according to his own feelings and opinions. From this beginning the two colors became the permanent badge of the two lines, so much so that artificial roses of red and white were manufactured in great numbers at last, to supply the soldiers of the respective armies.

But to return to the Duke of York. When it was found that he was advancing toward London, Somerset urged the king to put himself at the head of a body of troops and go out to meet him, and call him to account for his proceedings. The king did so, the queen accompanying the expedition. She was very anxious, and felt much alarmed for the safety of the king. After various marchings and manoeuvrings, the two armies came near each other in the county of Kent, to the southeastward of London. King Henry, who was eminently a man of peace, being possessed of no warlike qualities whatever, and being extremely averse to the shedding of blood, instead of attacking the Duke of York, sent a messenger to him to know what his intentions were in coming into the country at the head of such a force and what he desired.

The duke replied that he had no designs against the king, but only against the traitor Somerset, and he said that if the king would order Somerset to be arrested and brought to trial, he should be satisfied, and would disband his forces.

The king, on receiving this message, was much troubled and perplexed, but at length he concluded, under the advice of some of his counselors, to comply with this demand. He caused Somerset to be arrested, and notified the Duke of York that he bad done so. The Duke of York then disbanded his army, or at least sent the troops away; and made an appointment to come unattended and visit the king in his tent, with a view to conferring with him on the terms and conditions of a permanent reconciliation.

This interview resulted in a very extraordinary scene. It seems that the queen had contrived the means of secretly releasing Somerset after his arrest, and bringing him by stealth to the king's pavilion, and concealing him, there behind the arras at the time the Duke of York was to be admitted, in order that Somerset, might be a witness of the interview. While he was thus secreted, the Duke of York came in. He commenced, his conference with the king by repeating earnestly what he said before, namely, that he had not been actuated in what he had done by any feeling of hostility against the king, but only against Somerset. His sole object in taking up arms, he said, was that that arch traitor might be brought to punishment.

On hearing these words, Somerset could contain himself no longer, but, to the astonishment of the Duke of York and to the utter consternation of the king, he rushed out from his hiding-place, and began to assail the duke with the most violent reproaches, alleging that his pretensions of friendship for Henry were false, and that the real design of his movements was to usurp the throne. The duke retorted with equally fierce denunciations and threats. During the continuance of this altercation, the king remained stupefied and speechless, and at length, when the duke retired, officers were ready at the door to arrest him, having been stationed there by the queen.

He was held a prisoner, however, but a short time, for his son, who afterward became Edward IV., immediately commenced raising an army to come and release him. It was considered, for other reasons, dangerous to attempt to hold such a man in durance, since probably more than half the kingdom were on his side. So he was offered his liberty on condition that he would take the new and solemn oath of fealty to the king.

This he consented to do, and the oath was taken with great ceremony in St. Paul's Cathedral, and then he was dismissed. He went off to one of his castles in the country, muttering deep and earnest threats of vengeance.

It was about a year after this that Margaret's babe was born. It was a son.

Of course, the birth of this child immensely increased the difficulties and dangers in which the kingdom was involved, for it seemed to extinguish the hope that the quarrel would be settled by the York family succeeding peaceably to the crown on the death of Henry. Now, at length, there was an heir to the Lancastrian line. Of course Margaret, and all those who were connected with the Lancastrian line, either by blood or political partisanship, would resolve to support the rights of this heir. On the other hand, it was not to be supposed that the Duke of York would relinquish his claims, and he would no longer have any inducement to postpone asserting them. Thus the birth of the young prince was the occasion of plunging the country in new and more feverish excitement than ever. Plots and counter-plots, conspiracies and counter-conspiracies, were the order of the day. Every body was taking sides, or, at least, making arrangements for taking sides, as soon as the outbreak should occur. And no one knew how soon this would be.

The child was born on a certain religious holiday called St. Edward's day, and so they named him Edward. In a few months after his birth he was made Prince of Wales, and it is by this title only that he is known in history, for he never became king.

13

Illness of the King

THE circumstances of poor Margaret's case seem to have reversed all ordinary conditions of domestic happiness. The birth of her son placed her in a condition of extreme and terrible danger, while the immediate bursting of the storm was averted, and the sufferings which she was in the end called upon to endure in consequence of it were postponed for a time by what would, in ordinary circumstances, be the worst possible of calamities, the insanity of her husband. Happy as a queen, says the proverb, but what a mockery of happiness is this, when the birth of a child is a great domestic calamity, the evils of which were only in part averted, or rather postponed, by an unexpected blessing in the shape of the insanity of the husband and father.

Henry's health had been gradually declining during many months before the little Edward was born. The cares and anxieties of his situation, which often became so extreme as to deprive him of all rest and sleep, became, at length, too heavy for him to bear, and his feeble intellect, in the end, broke down under them entirely. The queen did all in her power to conceal his condition from the people, and even from the court. It was comparatively easy to do this, for the derangement was not at all violent in its form. It was a sort of lethargy, a total failure of the mental powers and almost of consciousness—more like idiocy than mania. The queen removed him to Windsor, and there kept him closely shut up, admitting that he was sick, but concealing his true situation so far as was in her power, and, in the mean time, carrying on the government in his name, with the aid of Somerset and other great officers of state, whom she admitted into her confidence. Parliament and the public were very uneasy under this state of things. The Duke of York was laying his plans, and every one was anxious to know what was coming. But Margaret would allow nobody to enter the king's chamber, under any pretext whatever, except those who were in her confidence, and entirely under her orders.

At length, about two months after Edward was born, the highest dignitary of the Church, the Archbishop of Canterbury, died. This event, according to the ancient usages of the realm, gave the House of Lords the right to send a deputation to the king to condole with him, and to ascertain his wishes in respect to the measures to be adopted on the occasion.

This committee accordingly proceeded to Windsor, and coming, as they did, under the authority of ancient custom, which in England, in those days, had even more than the force of law, they could not be refused admission. They found the king lying helpless and unconscious, and they could not obtain from him any answer to what they said to him, or any sign that the slightest spark of intelligence remained in his mind.

The committee reported these facts to the House of Lords. Finding how serious the king's illness was, the party of the Duke of York concluded to wait a little longer. There was a great probability that the king would soon die. The life, too, of the infant son was of course very precarious. He might not survive the dangers of infancy, and in that case the Duke of York would succeed to the throne at once without any struggle. So a sort of compromise was effected. Parliament appointed the Duke of York protector and defender of the king during his illness, or until such time as Edward, the young prince, should arrive at the proper age for undertaking the government. It was at this time that young Edward was made Prince of Wales. The conferring of this title upon him was confirmed by both houses of Parliament. They thus solemnly decreed that, though the Duke of York was to exercise the government during the sickness of the king and the minority of Edward, still the kingdom was to be reserved for Edward as the rightful heir, and he was to be put into possession of the sovereign power, either as regent in case his father should continue to live until that time, or as king if, in the interim, he should die.

The Duke of York and his friends acceded to this arrangement, in hopes that the prince never would arrive at years of discretion, but that, before many years, and perhaps before many months, both father and son would die. He thought it better, at any rate, to wait quietly for a time, especially as, during the period of this waiting, he was put in possession substantially of the supreme power.

Queen Margaret herself was extremely dissatisfied with the arrangement by which the Duke of York was made regent, since it of course deprived her of all her power. But she could do nothing to prevent it. Besides, her mind was so filled with the maternal feelings and affections which her situation inspired and with the care of the infant child, that she had for a time no heart for political contention.

Then, moreover, the Parliament, at the same time that they made the Duke of York regent, and thus virtually deprived the queen of her power, settled upon her an ample annuity, by means of which she would be enabled to live, with her son in a state becoming her rank and her ambition. One motive, doubtless, which led them to do this was to induce her to acquiesce in this change, and remain quiet in the position in which they thus placed her.

In addition to the liberal supplies which the Parliament granted to the queen, they made ample provision for maintaining the dignity and providing for the education of the young prince. Among other things, a commission of five physicians was appointed to watch over his health.

Margaret was the more easily persuaded to acquiesce in these arrangements from believing, as she did, that the state of things to which they gave rise would be of short duration. She fully believed that her husband would recover, and then the regency of the Duke of York would cease, and the king—that is, the king in name, but she herself in reality—would come into power again. So she determined to bide her time.

She accordingly retired from London, and set up an establishment of her own in her palace at Greenwich, where she held her court, and lived in a style of grandeur and ceremony such as would have been proper if she had been a reigning queen. Her old favorite, too, Somerset, was at first one of the principal personages of her court; but one of the first acts of the Duke of York's regency was to issue a warrant of arrest against him. The officers, in executing this warrant, seized him in the very presence-chamber of the queen. Margaret was extremely incensed at this deed. She declared that it was not only an act of political hostility, but an insult. She was, however, entirely helpless. The Duke of York had the power now, and she was compelled to submit.

But she was not required to remain long in this humiliating position. She procured the best possible medical advice and attendance for her husband, and devoted herself to him with the utmost assiduity, and, at length, she had the satisfaction of seeing that he was beginning to amend. The improvement commenced in November, about eight or ten months after he first fell into the state of unconsciousness. When at length he came to himself, it seemed to him, he said, as if he was awaking from a long dream.

Margaret was overjoyed to see these signs of returning intelligence. She longed for the time to come when she could show the king her boy. He had thus far never seen the child.

We obtain a pretty clear idea of the state of imbecility or unconsciousness in which he had been lying from the account of what he did and said at the interview when the little prince was first brought into his presence. It is as follows:

"On Monday, at noon, the queen came to him and brought my lord prince with her, and then he asked 'what the prince's name was,' and the queen told him 'Edward,' and then he held up his hands, and thanked God thereof.

"And he said he never knew him till that time, nor wist what was said to him, nor wist where he had been, while he had been sick, till now; and he asked who were the godfathers, and the queen told him, and he was well content.

"And she told him the cardinal was dead, and he said he never knew of it till this time; then he said one of the wisest lords in this land was dead.

"And my Lord of Winchester and my Lord of St. John of Jerusalem were with him the morrow after Twelfth day, and he did speak to them as well as ever he did, and when they came out they wept for joy. And he saith he is in charity with all the world, and so he would all the lords were. And now he saith matins of our Lady and even-song, and heareth his mass devoutly."

The very first moment that the king was able to bear it, Margaret caused him to be conveyed into the House of Lords, there to resume the exercise of his royal powers by taking his place upon the throne and performing some act of sovereignty. The regency was, of course, now at an end, and the Duke of York, leaving London, went off into the country in high dudgeon.

The queen, of course, now came into power again. The first thing that she did was to release Somerset from his confinement, and reinstate him as prime minister of the crown.

14

Anxiety and Trouble

FOR about six years after this time, that is, from the birth of Prince Edward till he was six years old, and while Margaret was advancing from her twenty-fourth to her thirtieth year, her life was one of continual anxiety, contention, and alarm. The Duke of York and his party made continual difficulty, and the quarrel between him, and the Earl of Warwick, and the other nobles who espoused his cause, on one side, and the queen, supported by the Duke of Somerset and other great Lancastrian partisans on the other, kept the kingdom in a constant ferment. Sometimes the force of the quarrel spent itself in intrigues, manoeuvres, and plottings, or in fierce and angry debates in Parliament, or in bitter animosities and contentions in private and social life. At other times it would break out into open war, and again and again was Margaret compelled to leave her child in the hands of nurses and guardians, while she went with her poor helpless husband to follow the camp, in order to meet and overcome the military assemblages which the Duke of York was continually bringing together at his castles in the country or in the open fields.

The king's health during all this period was so frail, and his mind, especially at certain times, was so feeble, that he was almost as helpless as a child. There was an hereditary taint of insanity in the family, which made his case still more discouraging.

Queen Margaret took the greatest pains to amuse him, and to provide employments for him that would occupy his thoughts in a gentle and soothing manner. When traveling about the country, she employed minstrels to sing and play to him; and, in order to have a constant supply of these performers provided, and to have them well trained to their art, she sent instructions to the sheriffs of the counties in all parts of the kingdom, requiring them to seek for all the beautiful boys that had good voices, and to have them instructed in the art of music, so that they might be ready, when called upon, to perform before the king. In the mean time they were to be paid good wages, and to be considered already, while receiving their instruction, as acting under the charge and in the service of the queen.

Margaret and the other friends of the king used to contrive various other ways of amusing and comforting his mind, some of which were not very honest. One was, for example, to have different nobles and gentlemen come to him and ask his permission that they should leave the kingdom to go and make pilgrimages to various foreign shrines, in order to fulfill vows and offer oblations and prayers for the restoration of his majesty's health. The king was of a very devout frame of mind, and his thoughts were accustomed to dwell a great deal on religious subjects, and especially on the performance of the rites and ceremonies customary in those days, and it seemed to comfort him very much to imagine that his friends were going to make such long pilgrimages to pray for him.

So the nobles and other great personages would ask his consent that they might go, and would take solemn leave of him as if they were really going, and then would keep out of sight a little while, until the poor patient had forgotten their request.

It is said, however, that one nobleman, the Duke of Norfolk, who was so kind- hearted a man that he went by the name of the Good Duke, actually made the pilgrimage to Jerusalem on this errand, and there offered up prayers and supplications at the famous chapel of the Holy Sepulchre for the restoration of his sovereign's health.

They used also to amuse and cheer the king's mind by telling him, from time to time, that he was going to be supplied with inexhaustible treasures of wealth by the discovery of the philosopher's stone. The philosopher's stone was an imaginary substance which the alchemists of those days were all the time attempting to discover, by means of which lead and iron, and all other metals, could be turned to gold. There were royal laboratories, and alchemists continually at work in them making experiments, and the queen used to give the king wonderful accounts of the progress which they were making, and tell him that the discovery was nearly completed, and that very soon he would have in his exchequer just as much money as his heart could desire. The poor king fully believed all these stories, and was extremely pleased and gratified to hear them.

There were times during this interval when the king was tolerably well, his malady being somewhat periodical in its character. This was the case particularly on one occasion, soon after his first recovery from the state of total insensibility which has been referred to. The Duke of York, as has already been said, was put very much out of humor by the king's recovery on this occasion, and by his own consequent deposition from the office of regent, and still more so when he found that the first act which the queen performed on her recovery of power was to release his hated enemy, Somerset, from the prison where he, the Duke of York, had confined him, and make him prime minister again. He very soon determined that he would not submit to this indignity. He assembled an army on the frontiers of Wales, where some of his chief strong- holds were situated, and assumed an attitude of hostility so defiant that the queen's government determined to take the field to oppose him.

So they raised an army, and the Duke of Somerset, with the queen, taking the king with them, set out from London and marched toward the northwest. They stopped first at the town of St. Alban's. When they were about to resume their march from St. Alban's, they saw that the hills before them were covered with bands of armed men, the forces of the Duke of York, which he was leading on toward the capital.

Somerset's forces immediately returned to the town. Margaret, who was for a time greatly distressed and perplexed to decide between her duty toward her husband and toward her child, finally concluded to retire to Greenwich with the little prince, and await there the result of the battle, leaving the Duke of Somerset to do the best he could with the king.

Very soon a herald came from the Duke of York to the gates of St. Alban's, and demanded a parley. He said that the duke had not taken arms against the king, but, only against Somerset. He professed great loyalty and affection for Henry himself, and only wished to save him from the dangerous counsels of a corrupt and traitorous minister, and he said that if the king would deliver up Somerset to him, he would at once disband his armies, and the difficulty would be all at an end.

The reply sent to this was that the king declared that he would lose both his crown and his life before he would deliver up either the Duke of Somerset or even the meanest soldier in his army to such a demand.

The Duke of York, on receiving this answer, immediately advanced to attack the town. For some time Henry's men defended the walls and gates successfully against him, but at length the Earl of Warwick, who was the Duke of York's principal confederate and supporter in this movement, passed with a strong detachment by another way round a hill, and through some gardens, and thence, by breaking down the wall which stood between the garden and the town, he succeeded in getting in. A terrible conflict then ensued in the streets and narrow lanes of the city, and the attention of the besieged being thus drawn off from the walls and the gates, the Duke of York soon succeeded in forcing his way in too.

King Henry's forces were soon routed with great slaughter. The Duke of Somerset and several other prominent nobles were killed. The king himself was wounded by an arrow, which struck him in the neck as he was standing under his banner in the street with his officers around him. When these his attendants saw that the battle was going against him, they all forsook him and fled, leaving him by his banner alone. He remained here quietly for some time, and then went into a shop near by, where presently the Duke of York found him.

As soon as the Duke came into the king's presence he kneeled before him, thus acknowledging him as king, and said,

"The traitor and public enemy against whom we took up arms is dead, and now there will be no farther trouble."

"Then," said the king, "for God's sake, go and stop the slaughter of my subjects."

The duke immediately sent orders to stop the fighting, and, taking the king by the hand, he led him to the Abbey of St. Alban's, a venerable monastic edifice, greatly celebrated in the histories of these times, and there caused him to be conveyed to his apartment. The next day he took him to London. He rendered him all external tokens of homage and obedience by the way, but still virtually the king was his prisoner.

Poor Queen Margaret was all this time at Greenwich, waiting in the utmost suspense and anxiety to hear tidings of the battle. When, at length, the news arrived that the battle had been lost, that the king had been wounded, and was now virtually a prisoner in the hands of her abhorred and hated enemy, she was thrown into a state of utter despair, so much so that she remained for some hours in a sort of stupor, as if all was now lost, and it was useless and hopeless to continue the struggle any longer.

She however, at length, revived, and began to consider again what was to be done. The prospect before her, however, seemed to grow darker and darker. The fatigue and excitement which the king had suffered, joined to the effects of his wound, which seemed not disposed to heal, produced a relapse. The Duke of York appears to have considered that the time had not yet come for him to attempt to assert his claims to the throne. He contented himself with so exhibiting the condition of the king to members of Parliament as to induce that body to appoint him protector again. When he had thus regained possession of power, he restored the king to the care of the queen, and sent her, with him and the little prince, into the country.

MARGARET OF ANJOU

One of the most extraordinary circumstances which occurred in the course of these anxious and troubled years was a famous reconciliation which took place at one time between the parties to this great quarrel. It was at a time when England was threatened with an invasion from France. Queen Margaret proposed a grand meeting of all the lords and nobles on both sides, to agree upon some terms of pacification by which the intestine feud which divided and distracted the country might be healed, and the way prepared for turning their united strength against the foe. But it was a very dangerous thing to attempt to bring these turbulent leaders together. They had no confidence in each other, and no one of them would be willing to come to the congress without bringing with him a large armed force of followers and retainers, to defend him in case of violence or treachery. Finally, it was agreed to appoint the Lord-mayor of London to keep the peace among the various parties, and, to enable him to do this effectually, he was provided with a force of ten thousand men. These men were volunteers raised from among the citizens of London.

When the time arrived for the meeting, the various leaders came in toward London, each at the head of a body of retainers. One man came with five hundred men, another with four hundred, and another with six hundred, who were all dressed in uniform with scarlet coats. Another nobleman, representing the great Percy family, came at the head of a body of fifteen hundred men, all his own personal retainers, and every one of them ready to fight any where and against any body, the moment that their feudal lord should give the word.

These various chieftains, each at the head of his troops, came to London at the appointed time, and established themselves at different castles and strong- holds in and around the city, like so many independent sovereigns coming together to negotiate a treaty of peace.

They spent two whole months in disputes and debates, in which the fiercest invectives and the most angry criminations and recriminations were uttered continually on both sides. At length, marvelous to relate, they came to an agreement All the points in dispute were arranged, a treaty was signed, and a grand reconciliation—that is, a pretended one—was the result.

This meeting was convened about the middle of January, and on the twenty-fourth of March the agreement was finally made and ratified, and sealed, in a solemn manner, by the great seal. It contained a great variety of agreements and specifications, which it is not necessary to recapitulate here, but when all was concluded there was a grand public ceremony in commemoration of the event.

At this celebration the king and queen, wearing their crowns and royal robes, walked in solemn procession to St. Paul's Cathedral in the city. They were followed by the leading peers and prelates walking two and two; and, in order to exhibit to public view the most perfect tokens and pledges of the fullness and sincerity of this grand reconciliation, it was arranged that those who had been most bitterly hostile to each other in the late quarrels should be paired together as they walked. Thus, immediately behind the king, who walked alone, came the queen and the Duke of York walking together hand in hand, as if they were on the most loving terms imaginable, and so with the rest.

The citizens of London, and vast crowds of other people who had come in from the surrounding towns to witness the spectacle, joined in the celebration by forming lines along the streets as the procession passed by, and greeting the reconciled pairs with long and loud acclamations; and when night came, they brightened up the whole city with illuminations of their houses and bonfires in the streets.

In about a year after this the parties to this grand pacification were fighting each other more fiercely and furiously than ever.

At one time, when the little prince was about six years old, the queen made a royal progress through certain counties in the interior of the country, ostensibly to benefit the king's health by change of air, and by the gentle exercise and agreeable recreation afforded by a journey, but really, it is said, to interest the nobles and the people of the region through which she passed in her cause, and especially in that of the little prince, whom she took on that occasion to show to all the people on her route. She had adopted for him the device of his renowned ancestor, Edward III., which was a swan; and she had caused to be made for him a large number of small silver swans, which he was to present to the nobles and gentlemen, and to all who were admitted to a personal audience, in the towns through which he passed. He was a bright and beautiful boy, and he gave these little swans to the people who came around him with such a sweet and charming grace, that all who saw him were inspired with feelings of the warmest interest and affection for him.

The Little Prince and his Swans

Very soon after this time the war between the two great contending parties broke out anew, and took such a course as very soon deprived King Henry of his crown. The events which led to this result will be related in the next chapter.

15

Margaret a Fugitive

IN the summer of 1459, the year after the grand reconciliation took place which is described in the last chapter, two vast armies, belonging respectively to the two parties, which had been gradually gathering for a long time, came up together at a place called Blore Heath, in Staffordshire, in the heart of England. A great battle ensued. During the battle Henry lay dangerously ill in the town of Coleshill, which was not far off. Margaret was at Maccleston, another village very near the field of battle. From the tower of the church in Maccleston she watched the progress of the fight. Salisbury was at the head of the York party. Margaret's troops were commanded by Lord Audley. When Audley took leave of her to go into battle, she sternly ordered him to bring Salisbury to her, dead or alive.

Audley had ten thousand men under his command. The soldiers were all adorned with red rosettes, the symbol of the house of Lancaster. The officers wore little silver swans upon their uniform, such as Prince Edward had distributed.

The queen watched the progress of the battle with intense anxiety, and soon, to her consternation and dismay, she saw that it was going against her. She kept her eyes upon Audley's banner, and when, at length, she saw it fall, she knew that all was lost. She hurried down from the tower, and, with a few friends to accompany her, she fled for her life to a strong-hold belonging to her friends that was not at a great distance.

The king, too, had to be removed, in order to prevent his being taken prisoner. He was, however, too feeble to know much or to think much of what was going on. When they came to take him on his pallet to carry him away, he looked up and asked, feebly, "who had got the day," but beyond this he gave no indication of taking any interest in the momentous events that were transpiring.

This defeat, instead of producing a discouraging and disheartening effect upon Margaret's mind, only served to arouse her to new vigor and determination. She had been somewhat timid and fearful in the earlier part of her troubles, when she had only a husband to think of and to care for. But now she had a son; and the maternal instinct seemed to operate in her case, as it has done in so many others, to make her fearless, desperate, and, in the end, almost ferocious, in protecting her offspring from harm, and in maintaining his rights. She immediately engaged with the utmost zeal and ardor in raising a new army. She did not trust the command of it to any general, but directed all the operations of it herself. There is not space to describe in detail the campaigns that ensued, but the result was a complete victory. Her enemies were, in their turn, entirely defeated, and the two great leaders, the Duke of York and the Earl of Warwick, were actually driven out of the kingdom. The Duke of York retreated to Ireland, and the Earl of Warwick went across the Straits of Dover to Calais, which was still in English possession, and a great naval and military station.

In a very, short time after this, however, Warwick came back again with a large armed force, which he had organized at Calais, and landed in the southern part of England. He marched toward London, carrying all before him. It was now his party's turn to be victorious; for by the operation of that strange principle which seems to regulate the ups and downs of opposing political parties in all countries and in all ages, victory alternates between them with almost the regularity of a pendulum. The current of popular sentiment, which had set so strongly in favor of the queen's cause only a short year before, appeared to be now altogether in favor of her enemies. Every body flocked to Warwick's standard as he marched northwardly from the coast toward London, and at London the people opened the gates of the city and received him and his troops as if they had been an army of deliverers.

Warwick did not delay long in London. He marched to the north to meet the queen's troops. Another great battle was fought at Northampton. Margaret watched the progress of the fight from an eminence not far distant. The day went against her. The result of the battle was that the poor king was taken prisoner the second time and carried in triumph to London.

The captors, however, treated him with great consideration and respect—not as their enemy and as their prisoner, but as their sovereign, rescued by them from the hands of traitors and foes. The time had not even yet come for the York party openly to avow their purpose of deposing the king. So they conveyed him to London, and lodged him in the palace there, where he was surrounded with all the emblems and marks of royalty, but was still, nevertheless, closely confined.

The Duke of York then summoned a Parliament, acting in the king's name, of course, that is, requiring the king to sign the writs and other necessary documents. It was not until October that the Parliament met. During the interval the king was lodged in a country place not far from London, where every effort was made to enable him to pass his time agreeably, by giving him an opportunity to hunt, and to amuse and recreate himself with other out-door amusements. All the while, however, a strict watch was kept over him to prevent the possibility of his making his escape, or of the friends of the queen coming secretly to take him away.

As for the queen and the little prince, none knew what had become of them.

When Parliament met, a very extraordinary scene occurred in the House of Lords, in which the Duke of York was the principal actor, and which excited a great sensation. Up to this time he had put forward no actual claim to the throne in behalf of his branch of the family, but in all the hostilities in which he had been engaged against the king's troops, his object had been, as he had always said, not to oppose the king, but only to save him, by separating him from the evil influences which surrounded him. But he was now beginning to be somewhat more bold.

Accordingly, when Parliament met, he came into London at the head of a body-guard of five hundred horsemen, and with the sword of state borne before him, as if he were the greatest personage in the realm. He rode directly to Westminster, and, halting his men with great parade before the doors of the hall where the House of Lords was assembled, he went in.

He advanced directly through the hall to the raised dais at the end on which the throne was placed. He ascended the steps, and walked to the throne, the whole assembly looking on in solemn awe, to see what he was going to do. Some expected that he was going to take his seat upon the throne, and thus at once assume the position that he was the true and rightful sovereign of England. He, however, did not do so. He stood by the throne a few minutes, with his hand upon the crimson cloth which covered it, as if hesitating whether to take his seat or not, or perhaps waiting for some intimation from his partisans that he was expected to do so. But for several minutes no one spoke a word. At length the Archbishop of Canterbury, who was in some respects the most exalted personage in the House of Lords, asked him if he would be pleased to go and visit the king, who was at that time in an adjoining apartment. He replied in a haughty tone,

"I know no one in this realm whose duty it is not rather to visit me than to expect me to visit him."

He then turned and walked proudly out of the house.

Although he thus refrained from actually seating himself upon the throne, it was evident that the time was rapidly drawing near when he would openly assert his claim to it, and some of the peers, thinking perhaps that Henry could be induced peaceably to yield, consulted him upon the subject, asking him which he thought had the best title to the crown, himself or the Duke of York.

To this question Henry replied,

"My father was king; his father was king. I have myself worn the crown for forty years, from my cradle. You have all sworn fealty to me as your sovereign, and your fathers did the same to my father and to my grandfather. How, then, can any one dispute my claim?"

What Henry said was true. The crown had been in his branch of the royal line for three generations, and for more than half a century, during all which time the whole nation had acquiesced in their rule. The claim of the Duke of York ran back to a period anterior to all this, but he maintained that it was legitimate and valid, notwithstanding.

There followed a series of deliberations and negotiations, the result of which was a decision on the part of Parliament that the Duke of York and his successors were really entitled to the crown, but that, by way of compromise, it was not to be in form transferred to them until after the death of Henry. So long as he should continue to live, he was to be nominally king, but the Duke of York was to govern as regent, and, at Henry's death, the crown was to descend to him.

The duke was satisfied with this arrangement, and the first thing to be done, in order to secure its being well carried out, was to get the little prince, as well as Henry, the king, into his possession; for he well knew that, even if he were to dispose of the old king, and establish himself in possession of the throne, he could have no peace or quietness in the possession of it so long as the little prince, with his mother, was at large.

So he found means to induce the king to sign a mandate commanding the queen to come to London and bring the prince with her. This mandate she was required to obey immediately, under penalty, in case of disobedience, of being held guilty of treason.

Officers were immediately dispatched in all directions to search for the queen, in order to serve this mandate upon her, but she was nowhere to be found.

16

Margaret Triumphant

THERE followed after this time a series of very rapid and sudden reverses, by which first one party and then the other became alternately the victors and the vanquished, through changes of fortune of the most extraordinary character.

At the end of the battle described in the last chapter, Margaret found herself, with the little prince, a helpless fugitive. There were only eight persons to accompany her in her flight, and so defenseless were they, and such was the wild and lawless condition of the country, that it was said her party was stopped while on their way to Wales, and the queen was robbed of all her jewels and other valuables. Both she and the prince would very probably, too, have been made prisoners and sent to London, had it not been that, while the marauders were busy with their plunder, she contrived to make her escape.

She remained a very short time in Wales, and then proceeded by sea to Scotland, where her party, and she herself personally, had powerful friends. By the aid of these friends, and through the influence of the indomitable spirit and resolution which she displayed, she was soon supplied with a new force. At the head of this force she crossed the frontier into England. The people seemed every where to pity her misfortunes, and they were so struck with the energy and courage she displayed in struggling against them, and in braving the dreadful dangers which surrounded her in defense of the rights of her husband and child, that they flocked to her standard from all quarters, and thus in eight days from the time that the mandate was issued from London commanding her to surrender herself a prisoner, she appeared in the vicinity of the city of York, the largest and strongest city in all the north of England, at the head of an overwhelming force.

The Duke of York was astounded when this intelligence reached him in London. There was not a moment to be lost. He immediately set out with all the troops which he could command, and marched to the northward to meet the queen. At the same time, he sent orders to the other leaders of his party, in different parts of England, to move to the northward as rapidly as possible, and join him there.

The duke himself arrived first in the vicinity of the queen's army, but he thought he was not strong enough to attack her, and he accordingly concluded to wait until his re-enforcements should come up. The queen advanced with a much superior force to meet him. The two armies came together near the town of Wakefield, and here, after some delay, during which the queen continually challenged the duke to come out from his walls and fortifications to meet her, and defied and derided him with many taunts and reproaches, a great battle was finally fought.

Margaret's troops were victorious. Two thousand out of five thousand of the duke's troops were left dead upon the field, and the duke himself was slain!

Margaret's heart was filled with the wildest exultation and joy when she heard that her inveterate and hated foe at last was dead. She could scarcely restrain her excitement. One of the nobles of her party, Lord Clifford, whose father had been killed in a previous battle under circumstances of great atrocity, cut off the duke's head from his body, and carried it to Margaret on the end of a pike. She was for a moment horror-stricken at the ghastly spectacle, and turned her face away; but she finally ordered the head to be set up upon a pole on the walls of York, in view of all beholders.

A young son of the duke's, the Earl of Rutland, who was then about twelve years old, was also killed, or rather massacred, on the field of battle, after the fight was over, as he was endeavoring to make his escape, under the care of his tutor, to a castle near, where he would have been safe. This was the castle of Sandal. It was a very strong place, and was in the possession of the Duke of York's party. The poor boy was cut down mercilessly by the same Lord Clifford who has already been spoken of, notwithstanding all that his tutor could do to save him.

Murder of Richard's Child

Other most atrocious murders were committed at the close of this battle. The Earl of Salisbury was beheaded, and his head was set up upon a pike on the walls of York, by the side of the duke's. Margaret was almost beside herself at the results of this victory. Her armies triumphant, the great leader of the party of her enemies, the man who had been for years her dread and torment, slain, and all his chief confederates either killed or taken prisoners, and nothing now apparently in the way to prevent her marching in triumph to London, liberating her husband from his thraldom, and taking complete and undisputed possession of the supreme power, there seemed, so far as the prospect now before her was concerned, to be nothing more to desire.

17

Margaret in Exile

BRIGHT as were the hopes and prospects of Margaret after the battle of Wakefield, a few short months were sufficient to involve her cause again in the deepest darkness and gloom. The battle of Wakefield, and the death of the Duke of York, took place near the last of December, in 1460. In March, three months later, Margaret was an exile from England, outlawed by the supreme power of the realm, and placed under such a ban that it was forbidden to all the people of England to have any communication with her.

This fatal result was brought about, in a great measure, by the reaction in the minds of the people of the country, which resulted from the shocking cruelties perpetrated by her and by her party after the battle of Wakefield. The accounts of these transactions spread through the kingdom, and awakened a universal feeling of disgust and abhorrence. It was said that when Lord Clifford carried the head of the Duke of York to Margaret on the point of a lance, followed by a crowd of other knights and nobles, he said to her,

"Look, madam! The war is over! Here is the ransom for the king!"

Then all the by-standers raised a shout of exultation, and began pointing at the ghastly head, with mockings and derisive laughter. They had put a paper crown upon the head, which they seemed to think produced a comic effect. The queen, though at first she averted her face, soon turned back again toward the horrid trophy, and laughed, with the rest, at the ridiculous effect produced by the paper crown.

The murder, too, of the innocent child, the duke's younger son, produced a great and very powerful sensation throughout the land. The queen, though she had not, perhaps, commanded this deed, still made herself an accessory by commending it and exulting over it, The ferocious hate with which she was animated against all the family of her fallen foe was also shown by another circumstance, and that was, that when she commanded the two heads, viz., that of the Duke of York and that of the Earl of Salisbury, to be set upon the city walls, she ordered that a space should be left between them for two other heads, one of which was to be that of Edward, the oldest son of the Duke of York, who was still alive, not having been present at the battle of Wakefield, and who, of course, now inherited the title and the claims of his father.

This young Edward was at this time about nineteen years of age. His title had been hitherto the Earl of March, and he would, of course, now become the Duke of York, only he chose to assume that of King of England. He was a young man of great energy of character, and he was sustained, of course, by all his father's party, who now transferred their allegiance to him. Indeed, their zeal in his service was redoubled by the terrible resentment and the thirst for vengeance which the cruelties of the queen awakened in their minds. Edward immediately put himself in motion with all the troops that he could command. He was in the western part of England at the tine of his father's death, and he immediately began to move toward the coast in order to intercept Margaret on her march toward London.

At the same time, the Earl of Warwick advanced from London itself to the northward to meet the queen, taking with him the king, who had up to this time remained in London. The armies of Warwick and of the queen came into the vicinity of each other not far from St. Alban's, before the young Duke of York came up, and a desperate battle was fought. Warwick's army was composed chiefly of men hastily got together in London, and they were no match for the experienced and sturdy soldiers which Margaret had brought with her from the Scottish frontier. They were entirely defeated. They fought all day, but at night they dispersed in all directions, and in the hurry and confusion of their flight they left the poor king behind them.

During the battle Margaret did not know that her husband was on the ground. But at night, as soon as Henry's keepers had abandoned him, a faithful serving-man who remained with him ran into Margaret's camp, and finding one of the nobles in command there, he informed him of the situation of the king. The noble immediately informed the queen, and she, overjoyed at the news, flew to the place where her husband lay, and, on finding him, they embraced each other with the most passionate tokens of affection and joy.

Margaret brought the little prince to be presented to him, and then they all together proceeded to the abbey at St. Alban's, where apartments were provided for them. They first, however, went to the church, in order to return thanks publicly for the deliverance of the king.

They were received at the door of the church by the abbot and the monks, who welcomed them with hymns of praise and thanksgiving as they approached. After the ceremonies had been performed, they went to the apartments in the abbey which had been provided for them, intending to devote some days to quiet and repose.

In the mean time the excitement throughout the country continued and increased. The queen perpetrated fresh cruelties, ordering the execution of all the principal leaders from the other side that fell into her hands. She alienated the minds of the people from her cause by not restraining her troops from plundering; and, in order to obtain money to defray the expenses of her army and to provide them with food, she made requisitions upon the towns through which she passed, and otherwise harassed the people of the country by fines and confiscations.

The people were at length so exasperated by these high-handed proceedings, and by the furious and vindictive spirit which Margaret manifested in all that she did; that the current turned altogether in favor of the young Duke of York. The scattered forces of his party were reassembled. They began soon to assume so formidable an appearance that Margaret found it would be best for her to retire toward the north again. She of course took with her the king and the Prince of Wales.

At the same time, Edward, the young Duke of York, advanced toward London. The whole city was excited to the highest pitch of enthusiasm at his approach. A large meeting of citizens declared that Henry should reign no longer, but that they would have Edward for king.

When Edward arrived in London he was received by the whole population as their deliverer. A grand council of the nobles and prelates was convened, and, after solemn deliberations, Henry was deposed and Edward was declared king.

Two days after this a great procession was formed, at the head of which Edward rode royally to Westminster and took his seat upon the throne.

Margaret made one more desperate effort to retrieve the fortunes of her family by a battle fought at a place called Towton. This battle was fought in a snow-storm. It was an awful day. Margaret's party were entirely defeated, and nearly thirty thousand of them were left dead upon the field.

As soon as the result was known, Margaret, taking with her her husband and child and a small retinue of attendants, fled to the northward. She stopped a short time at the Castle of Alnwick, a strong-hold belonging to one of her friends; but, finding that the forces opposed to her were gathering strength every day and advancing toward her, and that the country generally was becoming more and more disposed to yield allegiance to the new king, she concluded that it would not be safe for her to remain in England any longer.

So, taking her husband and the little prince with her, and also a few personal, attendants, she left Alnwick and crossed the frontier into Scotland, a fugitive and an exile, and with no hope apparently of ever being able to enter England again.

18

A Royal Cousin

AS soon as Margaret escaped to Scotland, far from being disheartened by her misfortunes, she began at once to concert measures for raising a new army and going into England again, with a view of making one more effort to recover her husband's throne. She knew, of course, that there was a large body of nobles, and of the people of the country, who were still faithful to her husband's cause, and who would be ready to rally round his standard whenever and wherever it should appear. All that she required was the nucleus of an army at the outset, and a tolerably successful beginning in entering the country. There were knights and nobles, and great numbers of men, every where ready to join her as soon as she should appear, but they were nowhere strong enough to commence a movement on their own responsibility.

One of the measures which she adopted for strengthening her interest with the royal family of Scotland was to negotiate a marriage between the young prince, who was now seven years old, and a Scotch princess. She succeeded in conditionally arranging this marriage, but she found that she could not raise troops for a second invasion of England.

In the mean time, she had sent three noblemen as her messengers into France, to see what could be done in that country. France was her native land, and the king at that time, Charles VII., was her uncle. She had strong reason to hope, therefore, that she might find aid and sympathy there. Toward the close of the summer, however, she received a letter from two of her messengers at Dieppe which was not at all encouraging.

The letter began by saying, on the part of the messengers, that they had already written to Margaret three times before; once by the return of the vessel, called the Carvel, in which they went to France, and twice from Dieppe, where they then were, but all the letters were substantially to communicate the same evil tidings, namely, that the king, her uncle, was dead, and that her cousin had succeeded to the throne, but that the new king seemed not at all disposed to regard her cause favorably. His officers at Dieppe had caused all their papers to be seized and taken to the king, and he had shut up one of their number in the castle of Arques, which is situated at a short distance from Dieppe. He had been apparently prevented, from imprisoning the other two by their having been provided with a safe-conduct, which protected them.

Furthermore, the writers of the letter bade the queen keep up good courage, and advised her, for the present, to remain quietly where she was. She must not, they said, venture herself, or the little prince, upon the sea in an attempt to come to France unless she found herself exposed to great danger in remaining in Scotland. They wished her to notify the king, too, who they supposed was at that time secreted in Wales, for they had heard that the Earl of March—they would not call him King of England, but still designated him by his old name—was going into Wales with an army to look for him.

They said, in conclusion, that as soon as they were set at liberty they should immediately come to the queen in Scotland. Nothing but death would prevent their rejoining her, and they devoutly hoped and believed that they should not be called to meet with death until they could have the satisfaction of seeing her husband the king and herself once more in peaceable possession of their realm.

But the reader may perhaps like to peruse the letter itself in the words in which it was written. It is a very good specimen of the form in which the English language was written in those days, though it seems very quaint and old-fashioned now. It was as follows:

"MADAM,—

Please your good God, we have, since our coming hither, written to your highness thrice; once by the carvel in which we came, the other two from Dieppe. But, madam, it was all one thing in substance, putting you in knowledge of your uncle's death, whom God assoil, and how we stood arrested, and do yet. But on Tuesday next we shall up to the king, your cousin-german. His commissaires, at the first of our tarrying, took all our letters and writings, and bore them up to the king, leaving my Lord of Somerset in keeping at the castle of Arques, and my fellow Whyttingham and me (for we had safe-conduct) in the town of Dieppe, where we are yet.

"Madam, fear not, but be of good comfort, and beware ye venture not your person, nor my lord the prince, by sea, till ye have other word from us, unless your person can not be sure where ye are, and extreme necessity drive ye thence.

"And, for God's sake, let the king's highness be advised of the same; for, as we are informed, the Earl of March is into Wales by land, and hath sent his navy thither by sea.

"And, madam, think verily, as soon as we be delivered, we shall come straight to you, unless death take us by the way, which we trust he will not till we see the king and you peaceably again in your realm; the which we beseech God soon to see, and to send you that your highness desireth. Written at Dieppe the 30th day of August, 1461.

"Your true subjects and liegemen,

"HUNGERFORD AND WHYTTINGHAM."

Margaret remained through the winter in Scotland, anxiously endeavoring to devise means to rebuild her fallen fortunes. But all was in vain; no light or hope appeared. At length, when the spring opened, she determined to go herself to France and see the king her cousin, in hopes that, by her presence at the court, and her personal influence over the king, something might be done.

The king her cousin had been her playmate in their childhood. He was the son of Mary, her father René's sister. Mary and René had been very strongly attached to each other, and the children had been brought up much together. Margaret now hoped that, on seeing her again in her present forlorn and helpless condition, his former friendship for her would revive, and that he would do something to aid her.

She was, however, entirely destitute of money, and she would have found it very difficult to contrive the means of getting to France, had it not been for the kindness of a French merchant who resided in Scotland, and whom she had known in former years in Nancy, in Lorraine, where she had rendered him some service. The merchant had since acquired a large fortune in commercial operations between Scotland and Flanders which he conducted. In his prosperity he did not forget the kindness he had received from the queen in former years, and, now that she was in want and in distress, he came forward promptly to relieve her. He furnished her with the funds necessary for her voyage, and provided a vessel to convey her and her attendants to the coast of France. She sailed from the port of Kirkcudbright, on the western coast of Scotland, and so passed down through the Irish Sea and St. George's Channel, thus avoiding altogether the Straits of Dover, where she would have incurred danger of being intercepted by the English men-of-war.

She took the young prince with her. The king it was thought best to leave behind.

So great were the number of persons dependent upon the queen, and so urgent were their necessities; that all the funds which the French merchant had furnished her were exhausted on her arrival in France. She found, moreover, that the three friends, the noblemen whom she had sent to France the summer before, and from whom she had received the letter we have quoted, had left that country and gone to Scotland to seek her. They had provided themselves with a vessel, in which they intended to take the queen away from Scotland and convey her to some place of safety, not knowing that she had herself embarked for France. They must have passed the queen's vessel on the way, unless, indeed, which is very probably the case, they went up the Channel and through the Straits of Dover, thus taking an altogether different route from that chosen by the queen.

When they reached Scotland they hovered on the coast a long time, endeavoring to find an opportunity to communicate with her secretly; but at length they learned that she was gone.

In the mean time, Margaret, having arrived in France, borrowed some money of the Duke of Brittany, in whose dominions it would seem she first landed. With this money Margaret supplied the most pressing wants of her party, and also made arrangements for pursuing her journey into the country, to the town in Normandy where her cousin the king was then residing.

It is said that, on arriving at the court of the king and obtaining admission to his majesty's presence, Margaret took the young prince by the hand, and, throwing herself down at her cousin's feet, she implored him, with many tears, to take pity upon her forlorn and wretched condition, and that of her unhappy husband, and to aid her in her efforts to recover his throne. But the king, with true royal heartlessness, was unmoved by her distress, and manifested no disposition to espouse her cause.

Louis XI., Margaret's Cousin

Some negotiations, however, ensued, at the close of which the king promised to loan her a sum of money—for a consideration. The consideration was that she was to convey to him the port and town of Calais, which was still held by the English, and was considered a very important and very valuable possession, or else pay back double the money which she borrowed.

Thus it was not an absolute sale of Calais, but only a mortgage of it, which the queen executed. But, nevertheless, as soon as this transaction was made known in England, it excited great indignation throughout the country, and seriously injured the cause of the queen. The people accused her of being ready to alienate the possessions of the crown, possessions which it had cost so much both in blood and treasure to procure.

Of course, the security which the king obtained for his loan was of a somewhat doubtful character, for Margaret's mortgage deed of Calais, although she gave it in King Henry's name, and was careful to state in it that she was expressly authorized by him to make it, was of no force at all so long as Edward of York reigned in England, and was acknowledged by the people as the rightful king. It was only in the event of Margaret's succeeding in recovering the throne for her husband that the mortgage could take effect. The deed which she executed stipulated that, as soon as King Henry should be restored to his kingdom, he would appoint one of two persons named, in whom the King of France had confidence, as governor of the town, with authority to deliver it up to the King of France in one year in case she did not within that time pay back double the sum of money borrowed.

He seemed to think that, considering the great risk he was taking, a hundred percent per annum was not an exorbitant usury.

19

Return to England

MARGARET found one friend in France, who seems to have espoused her cause from a sentiment of sincere and disinterested attachment to her. This was a certain knight named Pierre de Brezé. He was an officer of high rank in the government of Normandy, and a man of very considerable influence among the distinguished personages of those times.

Margaret had known him intimately many years before. He was appointed one of the commissioners on the French side to negotiate, with Suffolk and the others, the terms of Margaret's marriage, and he had taken a very prominent part in the tournaments and other celebrations which took place in honor of the wedding before Margaret left her native land. When he now saw the poor queen coming back to France an exile, bereft of friends, of resources, and almost of hope, the interest which he had felt for her in former years was revived. It is said that he fell in love with her. However this may be, it is certain that Margaret's great beauty must have had a very important influence in deepening the sentiment of compassion which the misfortunes of the poor fugitive were so well calculated to inspire. At any rate, Brezé entered at once into the queen's service with great enthusiasm. He brought with him a force of two thousand men. With this army, and with the money which she had borrowed of King Louis, Margaret resolved to make one more attempt to recover her husband's kingdom.

JACOB ABBOTT

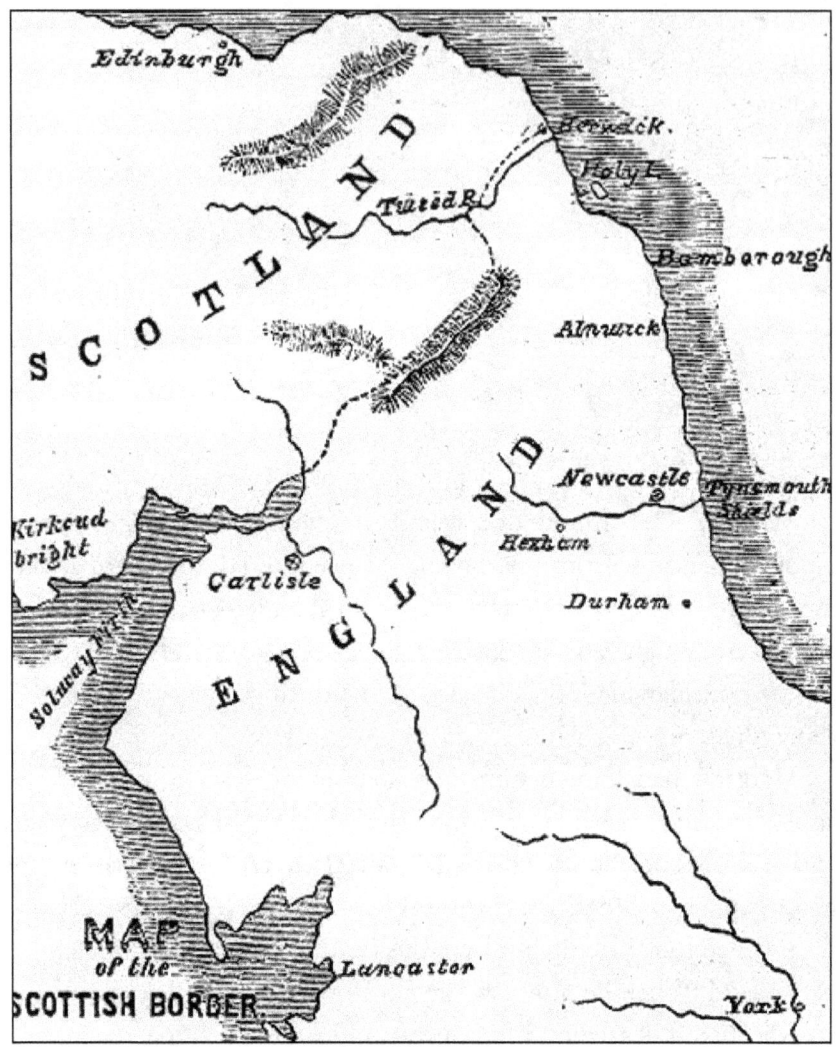

Map of the Scottish Border

At length, in the month of October, 1462, five months after she arrived in France, she set sail with a small number of vessels, containing the soldiers that Brezé had provided for her. Her plan was to land in the north of England, for it was in that part of the country that the friends of the Lancaster line were most numerous and powerful.

King Edward's government knew something of her plans, or, at least, suspected them, and they stationed a fleet to watch for her and intercept her. She, however, contrived to elude them, and reached the shores of England in safety.

The fleet approached the shore at Tynemouth, but the guns of the forts were pointed against her, and she was forbidden to land. She, however, succeeded, either at that place or at some other point along the coast, in effecting a debarkation; but she was threatened so soon with an attack by a large army which she heard was approaching, under the command of the Earl of Warwick, that the French troops fled precipitately to their ships, leaving Margaret, the prince, Brezé, and a few others who remained faithful to her, on shore. Being thus deserted, Margaret and her party were compelled to retreat too. They embarked on board a fisherman's boat, which was the only means of conveyance left to them, and in this manner made their way to Berwick, which town was in the possession of her friends.

They were long in reaching Berwick, being detained by a storm. The storm, however, caused Margaret a much greater injury than mere detention. The ships in which the French soldiers had fled were caught by it off a range of rocky cliffs lying between Tynemouth and Berwick, the most prominent of which is called Bamborough Head. The ships were driven upon the rocks and rocky islands which lay along the shore, and there broken to pieces by the sea which rolled in upon them from the offing. All the stores, and provisions, and munitions of war which Margaret had brought from France, and which constituted almost her sole reliance for carrying on the war, were lost. Most of the men saved themselves, and made their escape to an island that lay near, called Holy Island. But here they were soon afterward attacked by a body of Yorkist troops and cut to pieces.

Margaret reached Berwick in her fishing-boat at last, bearing these terrible tidings to her friends there. One would suppose that the last hope of her being able to retrieve her fallen fortunes would now be extinguished, and that she would sink down in utter and absolute despair.

But it was not in Margaret's nature to despair. The more heavily the pressure of calamity and the hostility of her foes weighed upon her, the more fierce and determined was the spirit of resistance which they aroused in her bosom. In this instance, instead of yielding to dejection and despondency, she began at once to take measures for assembling a new force, and the ardor and energy which she displayed inspired all around her with some portion of her confidence and zeal. A new army was raised during the winter. Very early in the spring it took the field, and a series of military operations followed, in which towns and castles were taken and retaken, and skirmishes fought all along the Scottish frontier. At length the contending forces were concentrated near a place called Hexham, and a general battle ensued. The queen's army was defeated. The king, who was in the battle, had a most narrow escape. He fled on horseback—for when he was in good bodily health he was an excellent horseman—but he was so hotly pursued that three of his body- guard were taken.

It is mentioned that one of the men thus taken wore the king's cap of state, which was embroidered with two crowns of gold, one representing the kingdom of England and the other that of France, the title to which country the English sovereigns still pretended to claim, in virtue of their former extended possessions there, although pretty much all except the town of Calais was now lost.

Perhaps the pursuers of the king's party were deceived by this royal cap; and took the wearer of it for the king. At any rate, the officer wearing the cap was taken, and the king escaped.

Immediately after the victory on the field at Hexham, a body of the Yorkist troops broke into the camp where the queen was quartered, and where, with the young prince, she was awaiting the result of the battle. As soon as the queen found that the enemy were coming, she seized the prince and ran off with him, in mortal terror, into a neighboring wood. She knew well that, if the child was taken, he would certainly be killed. Indeed, such bloody work had been made on both sides, with assassinations and executions during the year prior to this time, that men's minds were in the highest state of exasperation; and it is probable that both Margaret herself and the child would have been butchered on the spot if they had remained in the camp until the victorious troops entered it.

As soon as Margaret gained the wood she turned off into the most obscure and solitary paths that she could find, thinking of nothing but to escape from her pursuers, who, she imagined in her fright, were close behind. At length, after wandering about in this manner for some time, she fell in with a company of men in the wood, who were either a regular band of robbers, or were tempted to become robbers on that occasion by the richness of the stranger's dress, and by the articles of jewelry and other decorations which she wore; for, although Margaret's means were extremely limited, she still maintained, in some degree, the bearing and the appointments of a queen.

The men at once stopped her, and began to plunder her and the prince of every thing which they could take from them that appeared to be of value. As soon as they had possessed themselves of this plunder they began to quarrel about it among themselves. Margaret remained standing near, in great anxiety and distress, until presently, watching her opportunity, she caught up the prince in her arms and slipped away into the adjoining thickets.

She ran forward as fast as she could go until she supposed herself out of the reach of pursuit from the robbers, and then looked for a place in the densest part of the wood where she could hide, with the intention of remaining there until night. Her plan was then to find her way out of the wood, and so wander on until she should come to the residence of some one of her friends, who she might hope would harbor and conceal her.

She accordingly continued in her hiding-place until evening came on, and then, having recovered in some degree, by this interval of rest, from the excitement, fatigue, and terror which she had endured, she came out into a path again, leading little Edward by the hand. The moon was shining, and this enabled her to see where to go.

After wandering on for some time, she was alarmed by the apparition of a tall man, armed, who suddenly appeared in the pathway at a short distance before her. She had no doubt that this was another robber. It was too late for her to attempt to fly from him. He was too near to allow her any chance of escape. In this extremity, she conceived the idea of throwing herself upon his generosity as her last and only hope. So she advanced boldly toward him, leading the little prince by the hand, and said to him, presenting the prince,

"My friend, this is the son of your king! Save him!"

The man appeared astonished. In a moment he laid his sword down at Margaret's feet in token of submission to her, and then immediately offered to conduct her and the prince to a place of safety. He also explained to her that he was one of her friends. He had been ruined by the war, and driven from his home, and was now, like the queen herself, a wanderer and a fugitive. He had taken possession of a cave in the wood, and there he was now living with his wife as an outlaw. He led Margaret and the prince to the cave, where they were received by his wife, and entertained with such hospitalities as a home so gloomy and comfortless could afford.

Margaret remained an inmate of this cave for two days. The place is known to this day as Margaret's Cave. It stands in a very secluded spot on the banks of a small stream. The ground around it is now open, but in Margaret's time it was in the midst of the forest. The entrance to the cave is very low. Within, it is high enough for a man to stand upright. It is about thirty-four feet long, and half as wide. There are some appearances of its having been once divided by a wall into two separate apartments.

For two days Margaret remained in the cave, suffering, of course, the extreme of suspense and anxiety all the time, being in great solicitude to hear from her friends, the nobles and generals who had been defeated with her in the battle. Her host made diligent though secret inquiries, but could gain no tidings. At length, on the morning of the third day, to Margaret's infinite relief and joy, he came in bringing with him De Brezé himself, with his squire, whose name was Barville, and an English gentleman who had escaped with De Brezé from the battle, and had since been wandering about with him, looking every where for the queen. Margaret was for the moment overjoyed to see these friends again, but her exultation was soon succeeded by the deepest grief at hearing the terrible accounts they gave of the death of her nearest friends, some of whom had been killed in the battle, and others had been taken prisoners and cruelly executed immediately afterward. Up to this time, through all the danger and suffering which she had endured since the battle, she had been either in a state of stupor, or else filled with resentment and rage against her enemies, and she had not shed a tear; but now grief for the loss of these dear and faithful friends seemed to take the place of all other emotions, and she wept a long time as if her heart would break.

Margaret at the Cave

Margaret learned, however, from her friends that the king had made his escape, and was probably in a place of safety, and this gave her great consolation. It was thought that the king had succeeded in making his way to Scotland.

In the course of the day, one of the party who came with Brezé went out into the neighboring villages to see if he could learn any new tidings, and before long he returned bringing with him several nobles of high rank and princes of the Lancastrian line. Margaret felt much relieved to find her party so strengthened, and arrangements were soon made by the whole party for Margaret to leave the cave with them, and endeavor to reach the Scottish frontier, which was not much more, in a direct line, than thirty miles from where they were.

Before they departed from the cave Margaret expressed her thanks very earnestly to the outlaw and his wife for their kindness in receiving her and the little prince into their cave, and in doing so much for their comfort while there, although by so doing they not only encroached very much upon their own slender means of support, but also incurred a very serious risk in harboring such a fugitive. Having been plundered of every thing by the robbers in the wood, she had nothing but thanks to return to her kind protectors. The nobles who were now with her offered the wife of the outlaw some money—for they had still a small supply of money left—but she would not receive it. They would require all they had, she said, for themselves, before they reached Scotland.

The queen was much moved by this generosity, and she said that of all that she had lost there was nothing that she regretted so much as the power of rewarding such goodness.

On leaving the wood at Hexham, the party, instead of proceeding north, directly toward the frontier of Scotland, concluded to journey westward to Carlisle, intending to take passage by water from that place through Solway to Kirkcudbright, the port from which Margaret had sailed when she went to France. They were obliged to use a great many precautions in traversing the country to prevent being discovered. The party consisted of Margaret and the young prince, attended by Brezé and his squire, and also by the man of the cave, who was acquainted with the country, and acted as guide. They reached Carlisle in safety, and there embarked on board a vessel, which took them down the Firth and landed them in Kirkcudbright.

Though now out of England, Margaret did not feel much more at ease than before, for during her absence in France a treaty had been made between King Edward and the Scottish king which would prevent the latter from openly harboring her in his dominions; so she was obliged to keep closely concealed.

20

Years of Exile

MARGARET had not been long in Kirkcudbright before she was accidentally seen by a man who knew her. This man was an Englishman. His name was Cork. He was of the Yorkist party. He said nothing when he saw the queen, but he immediately formed the resolution to seize her and all her party, and to convey them to England and give them up to King Edward. He contrived some way to carry this plot into execution. He seized de Brezé and his squire, and also the queen and the prince, and carried them on board a boat in the night, having first bound and gagged them, to disable them from making resistance or uttering any cries. It seems that De Brezé was not with the queen when he was taken, and as it was dark when they were put on board the boat, and neither could speak, neither party knew that the others were there until the morning, when they were far away from the shore, out in the wide part of the Solway Bay.

In the night, however, De Brezé, who was a man of address and of great personal strength, as well as of undaunted bravery, contrived to get free from his bonds, and also to free his squire, without letting the boatmen know what he had done. Then, in the morning, watching for a good opportunity, they together rose upon the boatmen, seized the oars, and, after a violent struggle, in which they came very near upsetting the boat, they finally succeeded in killing some of the men, and in throwing the others overboard. They immediately liberated Margaret and the prince, and then attempted to make for the shore.

After having been tossed about for sometime in the Gulf or Firth of Solway, the boat was carried by the wind away up through the North Channel more than sixty miles, and finally was thrown upon a sand-bank near the coast of Cantyre, a famous promontory extending into the sea in this part of Scotland. The boat struck at some distance from the dry land, and the sea rolled in so heavily upon it that there was danger of its being broken to pieces; so De Brezé took the queen upon his shoulders, and, wading through the water, conveyed her to the shore. Barville, the squire, carried the prince in the same way. And so they were once more safe on land.

They found the coast wild and barren, and the country desolate; but this was attended with one advantage at least, and that was that the queen was in little danger of being recognized; for, as one of Margaret's historians expresses it, the peasants were so ignorant that they could not conceive of any one's being a queen unless she had a crown upon her head and a sceptre in her hand.

They all went up a little way into the country, and at length found a small hamlet, where Margaret concluded to remain with the prince until De Brezé could go to Edinburgh and learn what the condition of the country was, and so enable her to consider what course to pursue.

The report which De Brezé brought back on his return was very discouraging. Margaret, however, on hearing it, determined to go to Edinburgh herself, to see what she could do. She found, on her arrival there, that the government were not willing to do any thing more for her. They would furnish her with the means, they said, if she wished, of going back to England in a quiet way, with a view of seeking refuge among some of her friends there, but that was all that they could do.

So Margaret went back to England, and remained for some little time in the great castle of Bamborough, which was still in the hands of her friends. She tried here to contrive some way of reassembling her scattered adherents and making a new rally, but she found that that objest could not be accomplished. Thus all the resources which could be furnished by France, Scotland, or England for her failing cause seemed to be exhausted, and, after turning her eyes in every direction for help, she concluded to cross the German Ocean into Flanders, to see if she could find any sympathy or succor there.

Compared with the number of attendants that were with her in her flight into Scotland, the retinue of friends and followers by which she was accompanied in this retreat to the Continent was quite large, though it is probable that most of this company went with her quite as much on their own account as on the queen's. The whole party numbered about two hundred. They embarked from Bamborough on board two ships, but very soon after they had left the land a storm arose, and the two ships were separated from each other, and for twelve hours, the one which Margaret and the prince had taken was in imminent danger of being overwhelmed. The wind rose to a perfect hurricane, and no one expected that they could possibly escape.

At length, however, the gale subsided so as to allow the ship to make a port; not the port of their destination, however, but one far to the southward of it, in a territory belonging to Philip, Duke of Burgundy, between whom and Margaret there had been, during all Margaret's life, a hereditary and implacable enmity. Margaret was greatly alarmed at finding herself thus at the mercy of a person whom she considered as one of her deadliest foes.

But, very much to her surprise, the duke, as soon as he heard of her arrival in the country, took pity on her misfortunes, forgot all his former enmity, and treated her in the most generous manner. He was not at Lille, his capital, when she arrived, but he sent his son to receive her, and to conduct her to the capital, with every possible mark of respect. When she went on afterward to meet the duke, he sent a guard of honor to escort her, and when she arrived at his court, which was at that time at a place called St. Pol, he received her in a very distinguished manner, and prepared great entertainments and festivities to do her honor.

He rendered her, also, still more substantial services than these, by furnishing her with an ample supply of funds for all her immediate wants. He gave to each of the ladies in her train a hundred crowns, to Brezé a thousand, and to Margaret herself an order on his treasurer for ten thousand.

King René, Margaret's father, was very much touched with this generosity and kindness on the part of his old family enemy. He himself, at that time, was wholly destitute, and unable to do anything for his daughter's relief. He, however, wrote a letter of warm thanks to Philip, in which he declared that he had not merited, and did not expect such kindness at his hand.

We have in the conduct of the Duke of Burgundy on this occasion, one single and solitary example, among all the Christian knights, and nobles, and princes that figure in this long and melancholy story of contention, cruelty, and crime in which the Savior's rule, Forgive your enemies, do good to them that hate you, was cordially obeyed and what happy fruits immediately resulted to all concerned How much of all the vast amount of bloodshed and suffering which prevailed during these gloomy times would have been prevented, if those who professed to be followers of Christ had been really what they pretended.

With the money which Margaret obtained from the of Burgundy she was enabled to continue her journey in some tolerable, degree of comfort to the old home of her childhood in Lorraine. All that her father could do for her was to furnish her, a humble place of refuge in a castle at Verdun, on the River Moselle, which flows through the province. She went there, attended with a small number of followers, and here she remained, in utter seclusion from the world and almost forgotten, for seven long years.

During all this time she enjoyed the comfort and satisfaction of having her son, the prince, with her, and of watching his progress to manhood under her own personal charge and that of one or two accomplished men who still adhered to her, and who aided her in the education of her boy. She was, however, hopelessly separated from her, husband. For a long time she did not know what had become of him. During this time he was leading a very precarious and wandering life in England, going from one hiding-place to another, wherever his friends could most conveniently secrete him. At length, however; the heavy tidings came to the queen, in her retreat at Verdun, that her husband had been betrayed in one of his retreats, and had been seized and carried to London as a prisoner in a very ignominious manner. It was to have been expected that he would be immediately put to death; but, as a matter of policy, the York party thought it not best to proceed to that extremity, especially as all his kingly right would have immediately descended to his son, in whose hands, with such a mother to aid him, they would have become more formidable than ever. Thus, on many accounts, it was better for his enemies to allow the old king to live.

But very special precautions were taken by King Edward's government to prevent Margaret and the young prince from coming into England again. A coast guard was set all along the shore, and every one in England who was suspected of being in communication with the exiled queen was watched and guarded in the closest manner possible. Some were tortured and put to death in the attempt to force them to give up letters or papers supposed to be in their possession. A certain wealthy merchant of London was accused of treason, and very severely punished, simply because he had been asked to loan money to Margaret, and, though he refused to make the loan, did not inform the authorities of the application which had been made to him.

Among other examples of the shocking cruelty of which those in power were guilty, in their hatred of Margaret and her cause, it is said that one man, who was found out, as they thought, in an attempt to convey letters to and fro between Margaret and some of her friends in England, was torn to pieces with red-hot pincers in a fruitless attempt to make him confess who the persons were in England for whom the letters were intended. But he bore the torture to the end, and died without betraying the secret.

21

The Reconciliation with Warwick

IN the fall of 1469, Margaret's mind was aroused to new life and excitement by news which came from England that great opposition had gradually grown up in the realm against the government of Edward, that many of his best friends had forsaken him, and that the friends and partisans of the Lancaster line were increasing in strength and courage to such a degree as to make it probable that the time was drawing nigh when Henry might be restored to the throne. The most important circumstance connected with the change which had taken place was that the great Earl of Warwick, who had been the most efficient and powerful supporter of the house of York, and the most determined enemy of Margaret and Henry during the whole war, had now abandoned Edward, and had come to France, and was ready to throw all the weight of his power and influence on the other side.

Of course, these tidings produced a great excitement all over France. King Louis XI. was specially interested in them, as they afforded a hope that Margaret might regain her throne, and so be able to redeem her mortgage, or else deliver up to him the security; so he called a council at Tours to consider what was best to be done, .and he sent for Margaret at Verdun to come with the prince and. attend it. He also sent for René, her father, and other influential family friends. It is said that when Margaret arrived and met her father, she was so much agitated by the news, and by the hopes which it awakened in her bosom, that, in embracing him, she burst into tears from the excess of her excitement and joy.

But she could not endure the idea of a reconciliation with Warwick. At first she positively refused to see or to speak to him. When, however, at, length he arrived at Tours, the king introduced him into Margaret's presence, but for a longtime she refused to have any thing to do with him.

"She could never forgive him," she said. "He had been the chief author of the downfall of her husband, and of all the sorrows and calamities which had since befallen her and her son.

"Besides," she said, "even if she were willing to forgive him for the intolerable wrongs which he had inflicted upon her, it would be very prejudicial to her husband's cause to enter into any agreement or alliance with him whatever; for all her party and friends in England, whom Warwick had done so much to injure, and who had so long looked upon him as their worst and deadliest foe, would be wholly alienated from her if they were to know that she had taken him into favor, and thus she would lose much more than she would gain."

Warwick replied to this as well as he could, pleading the injuries which he had himself received from the Lancaster party as an excuse for his hostility against them. Then, moreover, he had been the means of unsettling King Edward in his realm, and of preparing the way for King Henry to return; and he promised that, if Margaret would receive him into her service, he would thenceforth be true and faithful to her as long as he lived, and be as much King Edward's foe as he had hitherto been his friend. He appealed, moreover, to the King of France to be his surety that he would faithfully perform these stipulations.

The King of France said that he would be his surety, and he begged that Margaret would pardon Warwick, and receive him into favor for his sake, and for the great love that he, the king, bore to him. He would do more for him, he added, than for any man living.

Margaret at last allowed herself to be persuaded, and Warwick was forgiven.

There were several other great nobles, who had come over with Warwick, that were received into Margaret's favor at the same time, and, when the grand reconciliation was completely effected, the whole party set out together to go down the Loire to Angers, where the Countess of Warwick, the earl's wife, and his youngest daughter, Anne, were awaiting them. The countess and Anne were presented to the queen, and a short time afterward Louis ventured to propose a marriage between Anne and Prince Edward.

Margaret received this proposal with astonishment, and rejected it with scorn. She said she could see neither honor nor profit in it, either for herself or for her son. But at length, after a fortnight had been spent in reasoning with her on the advantages of the connection, and the aid which she would derive from such an alliance with Warwick in endeavoring to recover her husband's kingdom, she finally yielded. She was influenced at last, in coming to this decision, by the advice of her father, who counseled her to consent to the match.

The parties united in a grand religious ceremony in the cathedral church of Angers to seal and ratify the covenants and agreements by which they were now to be bound.

There was a fragment of the true cross, so supposed, among the relics in the cathedral; and this was an object of such veneration that an oath taken upon it was considered as imposing an obligation of the highest sanctity. Each of the three great parties took an oath, in turn, upon this holy emblem.

First, the Earl of Warwick swore that he would, without change, always hold to the party of King Henry, and serve him, the queen, and the prince, as a true and faithful subject ought to serve his sovereign lord.

Next; the King of France swore that he would help and. sustain, to the utmost of his power, the Earl of Warwick in the quarrel of King Henry.

And, finally, Queen Margaret swore to treat the earl as true and faithful to King Henry and the prince, and "for his deeds past never to make him any reproach."

It was furthermore agreed at this time that Anne, the Earl of Warwick's daughter, who was betrothed to the prince, should be delivered to Queen Margaret, and should remain under her charge until the marriage should be consummated. But this, was not to take place until the Earl of Warwick had been into England and had recovered the realm, or the greater portion of it at least, and restored it to King Henry. Thus the consummation of the marriage was to depend upon Warwick's success in restoring Henry his crown.

Still, a sort of marriage ceremony, or, more strictly, a ceremony of betrothal, was celebrated at Angers between the prince and' his affianced bride a few days afterward, with great parade, and then Warwick, leaving his countess and his daughter behind with Margaret, set out for England with a troop of two thousand men which Louis had furnished him.

After Warwick had gone, Margaret remained at Angers for some weeks, and then set out for Paris, escorted by a guard of honor. Her party arrived at the capital in November, and Margaret, by Louis's orders, was received with all the ceremonies and marks of distinction due to a queen. The streets through which she passed were hung with tapestry, and ornamented with flags and banners, and with every other suitable decoration. The people came out in throngs to see the grand procession pass; for, in addition to the guard of honor which had conducted the party to the capital, all the great public functionaries and high officials joined in the procession at the gates, and accompanied it through the city, thus forming a grand and imposing spectacle.

Queen Margaret and her party were in this way conducted to the palace, and lodged there in great splendor. Their hearts were gladdened, too, on their arrival, by receiving the news that Warwick had landed in England, and had been completely successful in his undertaking. King Edward was deposed, and King Henry had been released from his imprisonment in the Tower and placed upon the throne.

Margaret, of course, at once determined that she would immediately make preparations for returning to England.

22

Bitter Disappointment

THE preparations which were required for Margaret and her company to return to England in suitable state seem to have consumed several months; for, although it was as early as November that the great entrance into Paris took place, and the news of Henry's restoration was received, it was not until February that the royal party were ready to embark. There were negotiations to be made, and men to be enlisted, and ships to be procured, and funds to be provided, and appointments to be decided upon, and dresses to be made, and a thousand questions of precedence and etiquette to be considered and arranged. At length, however, all was ready, and the whole company proceeded together to the port which had been selected as the place of embarkation. This port was Harfleur. Harfleur is situated on the coast of Normandy, near the more modern port of Havre.

When the time arrived for sailing, the weather looked very unfavorable; but Margaret, who had become weary with the delays by which her return had been so long postponed, and was very impatient to arrive in her own dominions again, ordered the ships to put to sea. Three times did they make the attempt, and three times were the ships driven back into port again. Many of her friends were greatly discouraged by these failures. Some said they thought that this continued resistance of the elements to her plans ought to be regarded as an indication of divine Providence that she was not to go to England at present, and they begged her to defer the attempt. Others thought that the contrary winds were raised by witches, and they began to devise measures for finding out who the witches were.

Margaret paid no attention to either of these suggestions, but persisted in her determination to sail the moment that the weather should allow. This delay was a source of great inconvenience to her, and it occasioned a good deal of expense; for, besides her own personal officers and attendants, Margaret had collected quite a large body of soldiers to cross the Channel with her, in order to re-enforce the armies of Warwick and of Henry. This was quite necessary; for, although Henry had been nominally restored to the throne, his enemies were yet in the field in considerable force, and Margaret was very desirous of bringing with her the means of helping to put them down. In deed, she knew that the situation of her husband was extremely precarious, and that the fortune of war might at any time turn against him. And this consideration made her extremely impatient at the delay occasioned by the weather at Harfleur. She did not know but that the king might even then be engaged in close conflict with his foes, and likely to be overwhelmed by them, and that her force, by being so long: delayed, would arrive too late to save him.

Alas for poor Margaret! It was, indeed, exactly so.

It was not until the 24th of March that it was possible to leave the port; but then, although the weather was by no means settled, the queen determined to wait no longer. The Countess of Warwick, who had been left in France when the earl her husband went to England, sailed from Harfleur at the same time with the queen, though in a different vessel. Her daughter, however, the prince regent's bride elect, went with the, queen.

The weather continued very boisterous after the fleet sailed, and as the gales which blew so heavily were from the north, the ships could make very little progress. They were kept beating about in the Channel, or lying at anchor waiting for a change of wind, for more than a fortnight. During all this time Margaret was kept in a perfect fever of impatience and anxiety.

At length, about the 10th of April, they reached the land at Weymouth.

After the ships entered the port, the space of a day or two was occupied in making preparations to land. Among these preparations was included the work of arranging apartments at an abbey in the vicinity of Weymouth to receive the queen and her attendants. In the mean time, the landing of the troops was pushed forward as rapidly as possible.

The ship in which the Countess of Warwick embarked had sailed in a different direction from Margaret's fleet, and it was not known yet what had become of her.

When at last the preparations were completed, the queen and her party went on shore and took up their abode in the abbey. Margaret's mind was intensely occupied with the arrangements necessary for marshaling her troops and getting them ready to march to the assistance of Warwick, when, to her amazement and consternation, she received news, on the very next day after she took up her abode in the abbey, that the party of King Edward had mustered in great force and advanced toward London, and that a battle had been fought at a place called Barnet, a few miles from London, in which Edward's party had been completely victorious.

The Earl of Warwick had been killed. King Henry her husband had been taken prisoner, and their cause seemed to be wholly lost.

Warwick had gone into the battle on foot, in order the more effectually to stimulate the emulation of his men, so that when, in the end, his forces were defeated, and fled, he himself, being encumbered by his armor, could not save himself, but was overtaken by his remorseless enemies and slain.

Death of Warwick

The terrible agitation and anguish that this news excited in the mind of the queen it would be impossible to describe. She fell at first into a swoon, and when at length her senses returned, she was so completely overwhelmed with disappointment, vexation, and rage, and talked so wildly and incoherently, that her friends almost feared that she would lose her reason. Her son, the young prince, who was now nearly nineteen years of age, did all in his power to soothe and calm her, and at length so far succeeded as to induce her to consider what was to be done to secure her own and his safety. To remain where they were was to expose themselves to be attacked at any time by a body of Edward's victorious troops and conveyed prisoner to the Tower.

There was another abbey at not a great distance from where Margaret now was, which was endowed with certain privileges as a sanctuary, such that persons seeking refuge there under certain circumstances could not be taken away. The name of this retreat was Beaulieu Abbey. Margaret immediately proceeded across the country to this place, taking with her the prince and nearly all the others of her party. Either on her arrival here, or on the way, she met the Countess of Warwick, who, it will be recollected, had left Harfleur at the same time that she did. The countess's ship had been driven farther to the eastward, and she had finally landed at Portsmouth. Here she too had learned the news of the battle of Barnet and of the death of her husband, and, being completely overwhelmed with the tidings, and also alarmed for her own safety, she had determined to fly for refuge to Beaulieu Abbey too.

The two unhappy ladies, who had parted, three weeks before, on the coast of France with such high and excellent expectations, now met, both plunged in the deepest and most overwhelming sorrow. Their hopes were blasted, all their bright prospects were destroyed, and they found themselves in the condition of helpless and wretched fugitives, dependent upon a religious sanctuary for the hope of even saving their lives.

23

Childless, and a Widow

MARGARET did not trust entirely for her safety to the sacredness of the sanctuary where she had sought refuge. She endeavored, by all the means in her power, to keep the place of her retreat secret from all but her chosen and most trustworthy friends. Very soon, however, she was visited by some of these, especially by some young nobles, who came to her exasperated, and all on fire with rage and resentment, on account of the death of their friends and relatives, who had been slain in the battle.

They found Margaret, however, in a state of mind very different from their own. She was beginning to be discouraged. The long continued and bitter experience of failure and disappointment, which had now, for so many years, been her constant lot, seemed at last to have had power to undermine and destroy even her resolution and energy. Her friends, when they came to see her, found her plunged in a sort of stupor of wretchedness and despair from which they found it difficult to rouse her.

And when, at length, they succeeded in so far awakening her from her despondency as to induce her to take some interest in their consultations, her only feeling for the time being seemed to be anxiety for the safety of her son. She begged and implored them to take some measures to protect him. They endeavored to convince her that her situation was not so desperate as she imagined. They had still a powerful force, they said, on their side. That force was now rallying and reassembling, and, with her presence and that of the young prince at their head-quarters, the numbers and enthusiasm of their troops would be very rapidly increased, and there was great hope that they might soon be able again to meet the enemy under more favorable auspices than ever.

But the queen seemed very unwilling to accede to their views. It was of no use, she said, to make any farther effort. They were not strong enough to meet their enemies in battle, and nothing but fresh disasters would result from making the attempt. There was nothing to be done but for herself and the young prince, with as many others as were disposed to share her fortunes, to return as soon as possible to France, and there to remain and wait for better times.

But the young prince was not willing to adopt this plan. He was young, and full of confidence and hope, and he joined the nobles in urging his mother to consent to take the field. His influence prevailed; and Margaret, though with great reluctance and many forebodings, finally yielded.

So she left the sanctuary, and, with the prince, was escorted secretly to the northward, in order to join the army there. The western counties of England, those lying on the borders of Wales, had long been very favorable to Henry's cause, and when the people learned that the queen and the young prince were there, they came out in great numbers, as the nobles had predicted, to join her standard. In a short time a large army was ready to take the field.

Margaret was at this time at Bath. She soon heard that King Edward was coming against her from London with a large army. Her own forces, she thought, were not yet strong enough to meet him; so she formed the plan of crossing the Severn into Wales, and waiting there until she should have a larger force concentrated.

Accordingly, from Bath she went down to Bristol, which, as will be seen from the map, is on the banks of the Severn, at a place where the river is very wide. She could not cross here, the lowest bridge on the river being at Gloucester, thirty or forty miles farther up; so she moved up to

Gloucester, intending to cross there. But she found the bridge fortified, and in the possession of an officer under the orders of the Duke of Gloucester, who was a partisan of King Edward, and he refused to allow the queen to pass without an order from his master.

It seemed not expedient to attempt to force the bridge, and, accordingly, Margaret and her party went on up the river in order to find some other place to cross into Wales. She was very much excited on this journey, and suffered great anxiety, for the army of King Edward was advancing rapidly, and there was danger that she would be intercepted and her retreat cut off; so she pressed forward with the utmost diligence, and at length, after having marched thirty- seven miles in one day with her troops, she arrived at Tewkesbury, a town situated about midway between Gloucester and Worcester. When she arrived there, she found that Edward had arrived already within a mile of the place, at the head of a great army, and was ready for battle.

There was, however, now an opportunity for Margaret to cross the river and retire for a time into Wales, and she was herself extremely desirous of doing so, but the young nobles who were with her, and especially the Duke of Somerset, a violent and hot-headed young man, who acted as the leader of them, would not consent. He declared that he would retreat no farther.

"We will make a stand here;" said he, "and take such fortune as God may send us."

So he pitched his camp in the park which lay upon the confines of the town, and threw up intrenchments. Many of the other leaders were strongly opposed to his plan of making a stand in this place, but Somerset was the chief in command, and he would have his way.

He, however, showed no disposition to shelter himself personally from any portion of the danger to which his friends and followers were to be exposed. He took command of the advanced guard. The young prince, supported by some other leaders of age and experience, was also to be placed in a responsible and important position. When all was ready, Margaret and the prince rode along the ranks, speaking words of encouragement to the troops, and promising large rewards to them in case they gained the victory.

View of Tewkesbury

Margaret's heart was full of anxiety and agitation as the hour for the commencement of hostilities drew nigh. She had often before staked very dear and highly-valued friends in the field of battle, but now, for the first time, she was putting to hazard the life of her dearly beloved and only son. It was very much against her will that she was brought to incur this terrible danger. It was only the sternest necessity that compelled her to do it.

When the battle began, Margaret withdrew to an elevation within the park, from which she could witness the progress of the fight. For some time her army remained on the defensive within their intrenchments, but at length Somerset, becoming impatient and impetuous, determined on making a sally and attacking the assailants in the open field.

So, ordering the others to follow him, he issued forth from the lines. Some obeyed him, and others did not. After a while he returned within the lines again, apparently for the purpose of calling those who remained there to account for not obeying him. He found Lord Wenlock, one of the leaders, sitting upon his horse idle, as he said, in the town. He immediately denounced him as a traitor, and, riding up to him, cut him down with a blow from his battle-axe, which cleft his skull.

The men who were under Lord Wenlock's banner, seeing their leader thus mercilessly slain, immediately began to fly. Their flight caused a panic, which rapidly spread among all the other troops, and the whole field was soon in utter confusion.

When Margaret saw this, and thought of the prince, exposed, as he was, to the most imminent danger in the defeat, she became almost frantic with excitement and terror. She insisted on rushing into the field to find and save her son. Those around found it almost impossible to restrain her. At length, in the struggle, her excitement and terror entirely overpowered her. She swooned away, and her attendants then bore her senseless to a carriage, and she was driven rapidly away out through one of the park gates, and thence by a by-road to a religious house near by, where it was thought she would be for the moment secure.

The poor prince was taken prisoner. He was conveyed, after the battle, to Edward's tent. The historians of the day relate the following story of the sad termination of his career.

When Edward, accompanied by his officers and the nobles in attendance upon him, covered with the blood and the dust of the conflict, and fierce and exultant under the excitement of slaughter and victory, came into the tent, and saw the handsome young prince standing there in the hands of his captors, he was at first struck with the elegance of his appearance and his frank and manly bearing. He, however, accosted him fiercely by demanding what brought him to England. The prince replied fearlessly that he came to recover his father's crown and his own inheritance. Upon this, Edward threw his glove, a heavy iron gauntlet, in his face.

The Murder of Prince Henry

The men standing by took this as an indication of Edward's feelings and wishes in respect to his prisoner, and they fell upon him at once with their swords and murdered him upon the spot.

Margaret did not know what had become of her son until the following day. By that time King Edward had discovered the place of her retreat, and he sent a certain Sir William Stanley, who had always been one of her most inveterate enemies, to take her prisoner and bring her to him. It was this Stanley who, when he came, brought her the news of her son's death. He communicated the news to her, it was said, in an exultant manner, as if he was not only glad of the prince's death, but as if he rejoiced in having the opportunity of witnessing the despair and grief with which the mother was overwhelmed in hearing the tidings.

Stanley conveyed the queen to Coventry, where King Edward then was, and placed her at his disposal. Edward was then going to London in a sort of triumphant march in honor of his victory, and he ordered that Stanley should take Margaret with him in his train. Anne of Warwick, her son's young bride, was taken to London too, at the same time and in the same way.

During the whole of the journey Margaret was in a continued state of the highest excitement, being almost wild with grief and rage. She uttered continual maledictions against Edward for having murdered her boy, and nothing could soothe or quiet her.

It might be supposed that there would have been one source of comfort open to her during this dreadful journey in the thought that, in going to the Tower, which was now undoubtedly to be her destination, she should rejoin her husband, who had been for some time imprisoned there. But the hope of being thus once more united to almost the last object of affection that now remained to her upon earth, if Margaret really cherished it, was doomed to a bitter disappointment. The death of the young prince made it now an object of great importance to the reigning line that Henry himself should be put out of the way, and, on the very night of Margaret's arrival at the Tower, her husband was assassinated in the room which had so long been his prison.

Thus all Queen Margaret's bright hopes of happiness were, in two short months, completely and forever destroyed. At the close of the month of March she was the proud and happy queen of a monarch ruling over one of the most wealthy and powerful kingdoms on the globe, and the mother of a prince who was endowed with every personal grace and noble accomplishment, affianced to a high-born, beautiful, and immensely wealthy bride, and just entering what promised to be a long and glorious career. In May, just two months later, she was childless and a widow. Both her husband and her son were lying in bloody graves, and she herself, fallen from her throne, was shut up, a helpless captive, in a gloomy dungeon, with no prospect of deliverance before her to the end of her days. The annals even of royalty, filled as they are with examples of overwhelming calamity, can perhaps furnish no other instance of so total and terrible reverse of fortune as this.

24

Conclusion

ON the day following the assassination of Henry, the body was taken from the Tower and conveyed through the streets of London, with a strong escort of armed men to guard it, to the Church of St. Paul's, there to be publicly exhibited, as was customary on such occasions. Such an exhibition was more necessary than usual in this case, as the fact of Henry's death might, perhaps, have afterward been called in question, and designing men might have continued to agitate the country in his name, if there had not been the most positive proof furnished to the public that he was no more.

The body remained lying thus during the day. When night came, it was taken away and carried down to Blackfriar's—a landing upon the river nearly opposite Saint Paul's. Here there was a boat lying ready to receive the hearse. It was lighted with torches, and the watermen were at their oars. The hearse was put on board, and the body was thus borne away, over the dark waters of the river, to the lonely village of Chertsey, where it had been decided that he should be interred.

JACOB ABBOTT

View of Chertsey

For some time after Henry's death Margaret was kept in close confinement in the Tower. At length, finding that every thing was quiet, and that the new government was becoming firmly established, the rigor of the unhappy captive's imprisonment was relaxed. She was removed first to Windsor, and afterward to Wallingford, a place in the interior of the country, where she enjoyed a considerable degree of personal freedom, though she was still very closely watched and guarded.

At length, about four years afterward, her father, King René, succeeded in obtaining her ransom for the sum of fifty thousand crowns. René was not the possessor of so much money himself, but he induced King Louis to pay it, on condition of his conveying to him his family domain.

The ransom was to be paid in five annual installments, but on the payment of the first installment the queen was to be released and allowed to return to her native land. It was stipulated, too, that, as a condition of her release, she was formally and forever to renounce all the rights of every kind within the realm of England to which she might have laid claim through her marriage with Henry. It might have been supposed that they would have required her to sign this renunciation before releasing her. But it was held by the law of England, then as now, that a signature made under durance was invalid, the signer not being free. So it was arranged that an English commissioner was to accompany her across the Channel, and go with her to Rouen, where he was to deliver her to the French embassadors, who, in the name of Louis, were to be responsible for her signing the document.

This plan was carried into effect. Margaret set out from the castle of Wallingford under the care of a man on whom Edward's government could rely for keeping a close watch over her, and taking care that she went on quietly through England to the port of embarkation. This port was Sandwich. Here she embarked on board a vessel, with a retinue of three ladies and seven gentlemen, and bade a final farewell to the kingdom which she had entered on her bridal tour with such high and exultant expectations of grandeur and happiness.

She arrived at Dieppe in the beginning of 1476, and proceeded immediately to Rouen, where the commissioner, who came to attend her, delivered her to the French embassadors appointed to receive her, and attend to the signing of the renunciation.

The document was written in Latin, but the import of it was as follows:

I, Margaret, formerly in England married, renounce all that I could pretend to in England, by the conditions of my marriage, with all other things there, to Edward, now King of England.

It cost Margaret no effort to sign this paper. With the death of her husband and her son all hope had been extinguished in her bosom, and life now possessed nothing that she desired. She signed this fatal document, renouncing not only all claims to be henceforth considered a queen, but all pretension that she had ever been one, with a passive indifference and unconcern which showed that her spirit was broken, and that the fires of pride and ambition which had burned so fiercely in her breast were now, at last, extinguished forever.

When the paper was signed Margaret was dismissed and left at liberty to go her own way to her native province of Anjou, where it was her intention to spend the remainder of her days. Her plan was to pass by the way of Paris, in order to see once more her cousin, King Louis, who had treated her with so much consideration and honor when she was on her way to England with a fair prospect of finding her husband upon the throne. But the case was different now, Louis thought, and instead of receiving kindly her intimation that she was intending to visit Paris on her way home, he sent her word that she had better not come, and advised her instead to make the best of her way to her father in Anjou.

He, however, as if to soften this incivility, sent an escort to accompany her in her journey home, but Margaret was so stung by her cousin's heartless abandonment of her in her distress that she resolved to accept no favor at his hands; so she refused the escort, and set out with her few personal companions alone.

This little blazing up of the old flames of pride and resentment in her heart came near, however, to costing Margaret her life, for she had not gone far on her journey before an emergency occurred in which an escort would have been of great service to her. It seems that when the English were driven out of Normandy, many families and some whole villages remained of people who were too poor to return. These people were now in a very low and miserable condition. They mourned continually the hard necessity by which they had been left without friends or protection in a foreign land; and they understood, too, that the first beginning of the abandonment of their possessions in France by the English was the cession of certain provinces by the government of Henry VI. at the time of that monarch's marriage with Margaret of Anjou, and that all the subsequent misfortunes of their countrymen in France, by which, in the end, the whole country had been lost, had their origin in these transactions.

Now it happened that Margaret, on her journey from Rouen to Anjou, stopped the first night at one of these villages. The people, seeing a party of strangers come to town, gathered round the inn at night from curiosity to learn who they might be. When they were informed that it was Margaret of Anjou, Queen of England, who had been banished from the kingdom, and was now returning home, they were excited to the highest pitch of anger against her as the author of all their sufferings. They made a rush into the house to seize her, and, if they had been successful, they would doubtless have killed her upon the spot. But some of the gentlemen who were in her party defended her sword in hand, and kept the mob at bay until she gained her apartment. They guarded her there until they could send for the authorities, who came and dispersed the mob. Margaret immediately returned to Rouen, willing enough now to accept of an escort. A proper guard was provided for her, and under the protection of it she set out once more on her journey, and this time went on in safety.

When Margaret at last reached her native country of Anjou, she was received very kindly by her father, and went to live with him in a castle called the castle of Reculée, situated about a league from Angers, the capital of the province.

Here she remained about four years. It was a very pleasant place. The castle was situated upon the bank of a river, and yet in a commanding situation, which afforded a pretty view of the town. There was a beautiful garden attached to the castle, and a gallery of painting and sculpture. Her father, King René, was a painter himself, and he amused himself a great deal in painting pictures to add to his collection or to give to his friends.

But Margaret could take no interest in any of these things. Her mind was all the time filled with bitter recollections of the past, which, even if she did not cling to and cherish them, she could not dispel. She dwelt continually upon thoughts of her husband and her child. She made ceaseless efforts to obtain possession of their bodies, in order that she might have them transported to Anjou, and, as she could not succeed in this, she paid annually a considerable sum to secure the services of priests to say masses over their graves in England, in order to secure the repose of their souls.

Indeed, the anguish and agitation which continually reigned in her heart preyed upon her like a worm in the centre of a flower. "Her eyes, once so brilliant and expressive," says one of her historians, "became hollow and dim, and permanently inflamed from continual weeping." Indeed, the whole mass of her blood became corrupted, and a fearful disease affected her once beautiful skin, making her an object of commiseration to all who beheld her.

She continued in this state until her father died. He, on his death-bed, committed her to the care of an old and faithful friend, who, after King René's decease, took her with him to his own castle of Damprierre, which was situated about twenty-five miles farther up the river.

But, though Margaret was treated very kindly by the friend to whom her father thus consigned her, she did not long survive this change. She died, and was buried in the cathedral at Angers, and for centuries afterward the ecclesiastics of the chapter, once every year, at the return of the proper anniversary, performed a solemn ceremony over her grave by walking round it with a slow and measured step, singing a hymn.

THE END

ABOUT JACOB ABBOTT

Jacob Abbott was born in Hallowell, Maine in 1803, the son of a minister and farmer. Even as a young boy, he showed academic promise and an interest in spiritual matters. After attending the Hallowell Academy, he was admitted to Bowdoin College at the age of 14.

At Bowdoin, Abbott studied classics and mathematics. He graduated second in his class in 1820 at the young age of 16. He was known as a serious and studious young man who strove for excellence.

After college, Abbott went on to study at Andover Theological Seminary with the intention of becoming a Congregationalist minister. However, his rigorous study habits and frail health caused him to abandon this pursuit after just two years.

Abbott was plagued by gastrointestinal issues and migraines throughout his life, likely exacerbated by the demanding academic environment. His poor health finally forced him to leave his ministerial studies and turn to the less stressful pursuits of writing and tutoring.

First, Abbott took a job as a professor of mathematics and natural philosophy at Amherst College in 1824. The following year, he married Harriet Vaughan and moved to Boston where he opened a school for young ladies. It was during this time that he began writing simple textbooks for teaching science, history and Christian values.

So while Abbott had aspired to be a minister, chronic health issues led him to find an alternate calling educating children through clear and engaging writing. This pivot would launch his successful career as one of the most famous children's authors of the 19th century.

In 1825, Abbott married Harriet Vaughan and soon after started his own school for young ladies in Boston. During this time, he began

ABOUT JACOB ABBOTT

writing educational books in a popular, simple style. His early works included the Mount Vernon Reader and The Young Christian.

Abbott gained fame with the Rollo series, first published in 1835. These stories followed a young boy named Rollo learning morals and virtues through his everyday adventures. The series was hugely popular and established Abbott's reputation as a gifted children's writer.

Other notable books by Abbott include the Franconia Stories (1853-1873), a 10-volume series about a brother and sister's adventures in the country, and the Marco Paul series (1853-1873), which followed a boy's travels around America learning about each state.

In all, Jacob Abbott wrote over 200 books, primarily for young readers. His works were praised for their ability to educate and impart moral lessons in an engaging, story-driven way. Though largely forgotten today, he was one of the most prolific and beloved children's authors of his era.

Abbott continued writing up until his death on October 31, 1879 in Farmington, Maine. His legacy lives on through his contributions to 19th century children's literature.

BIOGRAPHIES ABBOTT WROTE

A number of the books Abbott wrote were biographies of famous people. Famous characters covered in these books included:

Alexander the Great: This book provides a sweeping look at the life and achievements of Alexander III of Macedon, better known as Alexander the Great. It follows his early education by Aristotle, ascension to the throne after his father Philip II's assassination, and extensive military campaigns across Asia and northeast Africa. Abbott recounts Alexander's major battles against the Persians and annexation of their empire. The book also examines Alexander's tactics, military innovations, and creation of a Hellenistic empire stretching from Greece to India before his death at 32.

Alfred the Great: This biography focuses on Alfred's defense of the Kingdom of Wessex against Viking raids in 9th century England. It discusses how Alfred drove back the Great Heathen Army and then negotiated terms with the Vikings, designating parts of England for their settlement. Abbott also highlights Alfred's efforts to revive learning and education in England, as well as his codification of laws and strengthening of the Anglo-Saxon navy. The book frames Alfred as a scholarly, strategic and devout ruler whose achievements laid the foundation for a unified England.

King Charles I: This book looks at the reign of Charles I leading up to and during the English Civil War. It focuses on the religious and political conflicts between Charles I and Parliament, caused largely by

Charles' belief in divine right of kings and many unpopular, authoritarian policies. Abbott also examines Charles' refusal to compromise, leading to the war against Parliament's New Model Army and his eventual execution for treason in 1649 under Oliver Cromwell.

King Charles II: This biography deals with the restoration of the English monarchy under Charles II after the death of Oliver Cromwell. It follows Charles II's return from exile and re-establishment of royal power. However, Abbott also notes Charles' own conflicts with Parliament and religious controversies during his reign. The book discusses Charles' hedonistic lifestyle and many mistresses, but also his support for science, exploration and trade that helped expand the British Empire.

Cleopatra: This book examines Cleopatra VII's life and rule over ancient Egypt. Abbott chronicles Cleopatra's relationships and political alliances with Julius Caesar and Mark Antony, as she sought to maintain Egypt's independence from Rome. The biography highlights Cleopatra's intelligence, education and strategic skills in dealing with Rome. But it ultimately focuses on Cleopatra's downfall and suicide after Mark Antony's defeat by Octavian, leading to Egypt becoming a Roman province.

Cyrus the Great: This biography covers Cyrus II of Persia, founder of the Achaemenid Empire. Abbott traces Cyrus's rise from Persian prince, to revolt against the Medes, to conqueror of the Lydian and Babylonian empires. The book also examines Cyrus's leadership qualities and tolerant policies toward conquered peoples. It portrays Cyrus as a wise, inspirational leader who created the model of a centralized Persian state.

Darius: This book looks at the reign of Darius I, examining his consolidation of the Persian Empire through administrative reforms, development of infrastructure, and expansion of territory. Abbott discusses

Darius's division of the empire into provinces and implementation of a uniform tax system and coinage. The biography also covers his invasion of Greece which was thwarted at the famous Battle of Marathon. Overall, it presents Darius as an capable, pragmatic ruler under whom the Persian Empire reached its zenith.

Queen Elizabeth: This biography celebrates the long and prosperous reign of Queen Elizabeth I of England. Abbott focuses on Elizabeth's shrewd leadership, religious compromise, and patronage of the arts and literature that fostered English Renaissance culture. The book also highlights Elizabeth's naval defeat of the Spanish Armada which secured England's independence from Europe. Overall, Abbott portrays Elizabeth as a commanding, canny and popular female ruler who strengthened England as a major world power.

Genghis Khan: This book looks at the incredible rise of Temüjin, better known as Genghis Khan. It follows his hardships as an outcast youth to becoming the fearsome founder of the Mongol Empire. Abbott chronicles Genghis Khan's brilliant military tactics and utterly ruthless conquests that allowed the Mongols to dominate much of Asia and Eastern Europe. Overall it paints him as a complex figure--strategic genius but also brutal tyrant.

Hannibal: This biography focuses on the great Carthaginian general Hannibal Barca. It recounts his famous crossing of the Alps with war elephants and invasion of Italy during the Second Punic War against Rome. Abbott details Hannibal's victories in major battles like Cannae but also his eventual defeat by Scipio and exile. The book celebrates Hannibal's daring military prowess but also concession late in life that Rome could not be conquered.

Josephine: This book examines the life of Josephine Bonaparte from her aristocratic upbringing in Martinique to her marriage to Napoleon Bonaparte. It focuses on Josephine's time as Empress consort of France and her support for arts and education. But it also discusses Napoleon's eventual divorce from her due to dynastic pressures. Overall the book presents Josephine as an intelligent, compassionate woman who tempered some of Napoleon's ambition.

Julius Caesar: This traces Caesar's life from early military campaigns to dictator and eventual assassination. Abbott covers Caesar's conquest of Gaul, rivalry with Pompey, famously crossing the Rubicon and crowning as dictator. The biography also examines the conspiracy led by Brutus and Cassius to assassinate Caesar in order to save the Roman Republic. In all, the book presents Caesar as an unmatched military mind who irrevocably changed the Roman Empire.

Margaret of Anjou: This biography looks at Margaret of Anjou who became queen consort to England's King Henry VI. It focuses on the political intrigue and machinations Margaret became involved in to support her husband's reign during the War of the Roses. Abbott portrays Margaret as a fiercely devoted, cunning woman who backed the Lancastrians against factions like the Yorkists led by Richard Neville. Though she lost power, the book frames her as a dominant figure during the conflict.

Mary, Queen of Scots: This book examines the life of Mary Stuart who became Queen of Scotland as an infant. It follows her tumultuous reign marked by scandals and plots to overthrow her by Protestants. Her Catholicism also put her at odds with England's Elizabeth I. Abbott recounts Mary's forced abdication, escape to England, and eventual execution ordered by Elizabeth for plotting against her. Overall it presents a tragic figure whose life was marked by political and religious turmoil.

Nero: This biography looks at the notorious Roman emperor Nero. It explores his self-indulgent lifestyle and tyrannical rule marked by possible matricide and the brutal execution of Christians. Abbott also examines legends around Nero like his fiddling during the Great Fire of Rome. The book presents a despotic, unstable man who drastically weakened the Roman Empire.

Peter the Great: This book covers the reforms and policies of Peter the Great that rapidly westernized Russia. Abbott discusses Peter's extensive European travels as a youth and later programs to remake Russia's army, expand its naval fleet, and build a new capital in St. Petersburg. The biography also examines Peter's harsh, authoritarian approach to governing that consolidated his power. Overall it presents him as a pivotal, transformative tsar.

Pyrrhus: This examines the life and military exploits of Pyrrhus, king of Epirus. It focuses on his campaigns against Rome where he won major battles but suffered heavy losses, giving rise to the term "Pyrrhic victory." Abbott recounts Pyrrhus's struggles to build a Greek empire and failed invasion of Sicily against Carthage. Though a skilled commander, Pyrrhus ultimately failed to achieve lasting gains.

Richard I: This biography looks at the reign of Richard I, known as Lionheart. It focuses on Richard's leadership during the Third Crusade to recapture Jerusalem from Saladin. Abbott also details the legendary tales of Richard's bravery and valor in campaigns against France and during his imprisonment. Overall, the book presents Richard I as one of England's great warrior kings.

Richard II: This explores the reign and overthrow of King Richard II. Abbott covers Richard's despotic actions that led the nobles to revolt and install Henry IV, leading to Richard's imprisonment and likely murder. The biography presents a weak king whose tyranny and poor leadership during a peasant's revolt cost him power and his life.

Richard III: This delves into the controversial rule of Richard III. Abbott examines Richard's contested path to the throne and the disappearance of the Princes in the Tower which Richard likely ordered. It also portrays Richard's defeat at the hands of Henry Tudor at the Battle of Bosworth Field that ended the Wars of the Roses. Ultimately Abbott paints Richard III as willing to employ any means to gain and retain the English crown.

Romulus: This recounts the Roman legend of Romulus and Remus, twin brothers raised by a she-wolf who went on to found the city of Rome. Abbott covers the myths of the brothers' quarrel over leadership, with Romulus killing Remus and becoming Rome's first king and architect of its nascent political institutions. Though mythological, Romulus represents ancient Rome's founding origins and rise to power.

William the Conqueror: This biography follows William, Duke of Normandy's conquest of England in 1066 after victory at the Battle of Hastings. Abbott discusses William's reign as king where he consolidated control, introduced feudalism, and fused English and Norman culture. William is presented as a formidable, innovative Norman leader who irrevocably transformed Anglo-Saxon England.

Xerxes: This examines the reign of Xerxes I of Persia, known for his failed invasion of Greece. Abbott focuses on Xerxes's gathering of a massive army to crush Greek resistance, but defeat at Salamis ended his ambitions. The book covers later unrest and palace intrigue that clouded the end of Xerxes's reign. Overall he is portrayed as a rash ruler whose desire for conquest led to disaster for Persia.

www.ingramcontent.com/pod-product-compliance
Lightning Source LLC
Chambersburg PA
CBHW070058080526
44586CB00013B/1114